THEORY FOR ROCK & POP MUSICIANS

A Practical Introduction to Contemporary Music Theory

VOLUME 1

by ADAM SAUNDERS

Published by
Trinity College London Press Ltd
trinitycollege.com
Registered in England
Company no. 09726123

Copyright © 2024 Trinity College London Press Ltd
First impression, July 2024

Unauthorised photocopying is illegal
No part of this publication may be copied or reproduced in any
form or by any means without the prior permission of the publisher.

Cover artwork: Rod Steele
Illustrations and diagrams: Jim Treweek
Printed in England by Halstan & Co, Amersham, Bucks

Contents

About the Author 5
Introduction 6
Overview 7
How to Use This Book 7

1. Pulse and Rhythm 9

Pulse 9
Rhythm 11
Noteheads, Stems, Tails & Beams 15
Rests 22
Dots 29
Ties 33
Time Signatures 36

2. Musical Building Blocks 40

The Musical Alphabet 40
The Stave 42
Clefs 43
   The Treble Clef 43
   The Bass Clef 45
   Drum Clef 48
   Tablature 48
Sharps, Flats, and Naturals 50
   Enharmonic Equivalents 51
Tones and Semitones 54
   Semitones 54
   Tones 56
Scales 58
   The Major Scale Formula 58
Degrees of the Scale 61
Intervals 64
   Interval Size 64
   Interval Type 68
   Lowering/Raising a Major Interval 70
   Lowering/Raising a Perfect Interval 74
The Circle of Fifths 80
Key Signatures 83
   Why Use a Key Signature? 83
   The Key Signature Clock 84
   Key Signature Hand Signals 86
   The Order of Sharps 88
   The Order of Flats 90
   Major vs Minor 94
   Finding the Relative Minor 96

The Natural Minor Formula ... 99
Minor Key Signatures ... 101

3. Harmony ... 103

Triads ... 103
Major Triads ... 103
Chord Symbols ... 103
Minor Triads ... 105

Sus2 and Sus4 Triads ... 109
Sus2 ... 109
Sus4 ... 109

Triads Within a Major Key ... 112
Diatonic Chords ... 112
Roman Numerals ... 112

Chord Progressions ... 115
Chord I ... 115
Chords I & V ... 117

Cadences ... 119
Perfect Cadence ... 119
Imperfect Cadence ... 119
Chords I & IV ... 120
Plagal Cadence ... 121
Chords I, IV & V ... 123
Chord vi (The Relative Minor) ... 126

The 12-Bar Blues ... 130
Standard 12-Bar Blues ... 130
Quick-Change Variation ... 131
Long V Chord Variation ... 132
ii-V-I Variation ... 133

4. Melody ... 139

Melodic Movement ... 139
Steps vs Leaps ... 140
Steps ... 140
Leaps ... 143
Pentatonic Melodies ... 146
Call and Response Melodies ... 150
Conclusion ... 154

Appendix ... 155

Keyboard Diagram ... 155
Major Scales – Treble Clef ... 156
Major Scales – Bass Clef ... 157
Natural Minor Scales – Treble Clef ... 158
Natural Minor Scales – Bass Clef ... 159
Manuscript Paper ... 160
Glossary ... 163
Recording Credits and Track Listing ... 166

About the Author

Adam Saunders is a keys player, producer, songwriter, and educator based in London, UK.

Adam co-developed the BA Music Performance and Industry course at Trinity Laban Conservatoire of Music and Dance, the first popular music programme for a London conservatoire. At Trinity Laban, Adam is Deputy Head of Popular Music and Module Leader for Musicianship. He has appeared as a keynote speaker at national and international music conferences and is a consultant for Trinity College London, Sing Up, and the Abram Wilson Charity.

Adam thrives on large-scale collaborations – his co-written musical, *Thames Tales*, was performed at the Royal Albert Hall by a cast of over a thousand.

As a media composer, his music has been played on television and radio networks worldwide, and he has composed and arranged tracks for brands such as Amazon, Aldi, and Barclays. Adam is one of the pianists featured on DECCA records's 'Music Lab Collective' and he has performed at many of the UK's most iconic venues including the Royal Festival Hall, Ronnie Scott's Jazz Club, the Camden Roundhouse, and the Hammersmith Apollo.

Adam is the founder of 'The Keys Coach – The Ultimate Online Piano Academy'.

Photography by Felipe Pagani

www.adamsaundersmusic.com

www.thekeyscoach.com

Introduction

There are many different approaches to learning popular music. While some people take one-to-one or group lessons with a teacher, others are self-taught or learn through YouTube and similar online platforms. Unlike classical music and jazz, there isn't so much of a standard pathway for learning popular music. Often people must find their own way and develop an approach that works best for them.

We have to forge our own pathways and, as a result, sometimes it can feel like we have gaps in our knowledge. It can also mean that the terminology we use when referring to elements of music can be different from person to person. For example, guitarists in rock bands will sometimes refer to playing a chord sequence 'four times' and might be unaware of the larger context of the structure. In blues, musicians often refer to a 'quick change', meaning playing chord IV in the second bar of a 12-bar blues. When you're starting out, it can be overwhelming to hear all this different language and it can be difficult to understand what it means.

This book aims to provide a standardised approach to music theory and terminology, allowing for more seamless communication between musicians.

Having said this, some of the most iconic musicians have very little understanding of music theory – it does not necessarily make you a better performer, songwriter, or producer. When The Kinks got together in 1964 to record 'You Really Got Me', arguably one of the most famous Rock songs of all time, I'm sure they didn't set out with the intention to write a song using the Mixolydian mode – it just so happens that without realising it, that's what they ended up doing!

However, when you have a solid foundation in music theory, you are equipped with a toolbox that you can refer to when practising, writing songs, performing, or producing. By understanding the building blocks of music, and recognising patterns and common sounds in the music you play, you can expand your horizons, develop a deeper knowledge of the music you like, and it will also give you the confidence to articulate your ideas clearly to others, who may be from completely different musical worlds.

When everyone speaks the same language, there are far fewer obstacles in the way of creativity.

Overview

This book will provide you with a clear understanding of the fundamentals of popular music theory, accelerate your aural skills, and take your musicianship to the next level. It will demystify the key terms related to harmony, melody, rhythm, and structure through practical exercises and audio tracks. It covers concepts related to drums, bass, guitar, keyboard, and vocals and is suitable for every contemporary musician.

This is the book for you if:

- interested in exploring the musical concepts and theories underpinning contemporary music
- taking a graded Rock & Pop exam and looking to further develop your understanding of the theory behind the repertoire
- studying Music or Music Technology in secondary, further, or vocational education
- aspiring to study popular music at university and want to understand the essentials to help you prepare for auditions and entrance exams
- a classically trained musician or music teacher and want to widen your knowledge of popular music theory.

Music theory can be a daunting term... but it doesn't need to be! This book will give you a solid foundation, accelerate your aural skills, and help take your musicianship to the next level.

How to Use This Book

The best piece of advice I can give you for using this book – **don't just read it!** Music theory isn't a subject that only exists on paper – it should be played, experienced, and explored on your instrument. To get the most out of this book, sit with your instrument and work through the material by physically singing or playing it.

If you're a singer, or drummer, and don't play a harmony instrument (keys or guitar), it would be useful in the long term to develop an understanding of how these instruments work as they are fantastic visual maps of how pitches are organised. This does not necessarily mean that you need to have keyboard or guitar lessons, but it is useful to at least know the notes on the keyboard or fretboard. If you don't have a keyboard or guitar, there are several free apps you can download which simulate these instruments so you can begin to make the connection between the theory and sound.

Physically singing or playing through the examples in this book will help you make connections between areas of understanding. If you don't make these links, there's a risk that there will be a separation between what you know on paper and what you play and practise.

You don't have to read the book from start to finish; feel free to jump to the sections that relate to the music you're currently working on. **The supporting audio tracks are the most important aspect of this book** – they will develop those important aural skills and help you connect how the topics sound, as well as how they are written on paper.

British musicians often use different terminology to American musicians when describing certain aspects of music theory. In this book, we'll use British terminology throughout. However, whenever a new concept is introduced, the American terminology will be in brackets to help you connect the two systems effectively.

There are several icons used throughout the book to help guide you through the topics.

Audio Tracks: the audio tracks will help to develop your aural skills and contextualise many of the concepts. Make sure you have a media player and a pair of headphones or speakers ready. I'd advise you to listen to each track several times before moving on.

Exercises: throughout the book there are practical exercises to test your understanding. The answers can be found online, see below for details.

Playlist: it's important to hear these theoretical concepts in real songs! The playlists will provide real-life examples of the topics covered. There is a QR code to scan for each list, but if you cannot access Spotify or a song becomes unavailable, the tracks have also been listed in each section.

Extra Info: these sections provide more detail about a specific topic.

Spotlight: sometimes music theory can be a little confusing and these sections aim to help demystify some of those more challenging concepts.

Summary: many sections include a summary where the main learning is recapped in order to refresh your memory and draw attention to any gaps in your understanding.

Questions: there are some written questions throughout the book that test your understanding of the terminology.

Accessing Playlists, Answers, and Audio

Playlists: access the Spotify playlists via the QR codes, or search for:

1) 'In the Pocket' Grooves
2) 4/4 Time Signature
3) 3/4 Time Signature
4) 2/4 Time Signature
5) Songs in a Major Key
6) Songs in a Minor Key
7) Chord I
8) Chords I and V
9) Chords I and IV
10) Chords I, IV and V
11) Chords I, IV, V and vi
12) 12 Bar Blues
13) Major Pentatonic Melodies
14) Call and Response Melodies

Answers: a PDF of answers can be downloaded from trinitycollege.com/answers-vol-1
It is also included in the audio download zip file.

Audio: can be downloaded using the code in the back of the book.

Pulse and Rhythm

Pulse

Let's begin with the most fundamental element of music – the pulse. Think of the pulse as like a musical heartbeat or a ticking clock – it's consistent and keeps on going throughout a piece of music. Listen to this track of a drummer playing a groove. They are playing with a really strong sense of pulse. In popular music, we often use the term groove to describe how the music moves and feels; the pulse is an integral part of this.

 1.01 Drum Groove

These pulse beats can be grouped into blocks – we call these bars [GB] (or measures [US]). In the diagram below, four pulse beats have been grouped together, separated by a barline. It's possible to have any number of beats in a bar, however, for the moment, we'll focus on the most common – four beats in a bar.

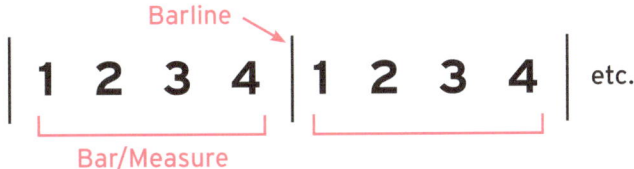

Listen to this track of the same drum beat with the pulse beats being counted out loud. Hear how the pulse beats connect to what the drummer is playing – the drum groove is locked in with the pulse beats.

 1.02 Drum Groove with Counting

When the groove is solid and has a good feel, this is sometimes referred to as being 'in the pocket'. Musicians who play 'pocket' are also described as having a good sense of 'time'. When a musician plays with a good sense of time, it can feel great and make you want to move! Playlists will appear throughout the book to underpin what is being said with real-life songs.

Playlist: 'In The Pocket' Grooves

This playlist features a variety of musical styles, showcasing iconic grooves that hopefully make you want to move!

- Funkadelic: Nappy Dugout
- The Meters: Cissy Strut
- Stevie Wonder: Superstition
- AC/DC: You Shook Me All Night Long
- Bruce Springsteen: Born In The U.S.A.
- Oscar Peterson Trio: C Jam Blues
- Chaka Khan: I'm Every Woman
- Bob Marley & The Wailers: Jamming
- Tower Of Power: What Is Hip?
- Crazy In Love: Beyoncé, Jay Z
- Think: Aretha Franklin

The speed of the pulse is known as the tempo. Popular music often measures tempo in Beats Per Minute (BPM) – the higher the BPM, the faster the tempo. For example, Beyonce's 'Love on Top' has a BPM of 99 meaning that there are 99 pulse beats per minute. Queen's 'Another One Bites the Dust' has a BPM of 110 meaning that this track has a faster tempo than Beyonce's. So a BPM of 60 would mean that each beat would be exactly one second long.

To work out the BPM of a piece of music you can either use a metronome or a smartphone app.

Extra Info: Metronome

A metronome is a device that produces a steady pulse beat. Mechanical metronomes are used to control the tempo by using a weight on a pendulum to increase or decrease the tempo.

Nowadays, musicians tend to use apps such as 'The Metronome' by Soundbrenner or 'Metronome Beats'.

Many apps allow you to manually tap in a tempo so you can work out the BPM of a song by tapping along to the pulse beats.

Exercise: What is the BPM?

Listen to the following drum grooves and work out the BPM. Begin by counting, or clapping along with the pulse, then use a metronome or smartphone app to help you find the BPM.

1.03 What's the BPM?......................

1.04 What's the BPM?......................

1.05 What's the BPM?......................

Answers can be found online, see page 8 for details.

Rhythm

Within each bar, we can add notes that sit on top of the underlying pulse – these notes form a rhythm.

Notes can have different lengths, and this is called their note value. A note held for one beat is called a crotchet (or quarter note).

Here are four crotchets in one bar:

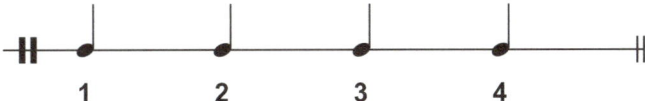

Notes can also fall in between each beat, and if we divide each beat into two, these are called quavers (or eighth-notes). Two quavers last for the same amount of time as one crotchet and musicians often count quavers using the number of the pulses, followed by an 'and' (+).

Here are eight quavers in one bar:

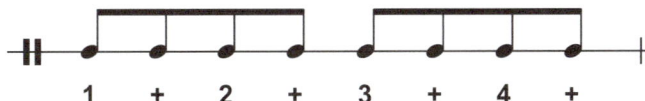

If we divide each beat into four we get semiquavers (or 16th-notes). Musicians often count four semiquavers using the number of the beat followed by 'e and (+) a'. We know they are semiquavers because they have two lines at the top connecting them.

Here are 16 semiquavers in one bar:

Listen to this track which demonstrates all these different note values being performed. The track begins with a spoken '1, 2, 3, 4' – this is called a count-in (or count-off). Count-ins help everyone in the band begin at the same time.

 1.06 Crotchet, Quaver, and Semiquaver Note Values

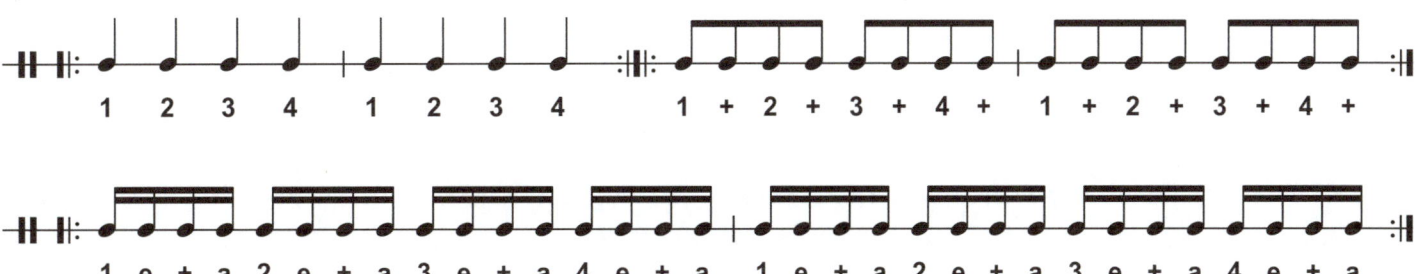

We can mix and match note values to create more interesting rhythms. Have a look at the example below which contains crotchets, quavers, and semiquavers. Listen to this rhythm being performed – the rhythm is played through twice.

 1.07 Crotchet, Quaver, and Semiquaver Rhythm

To work out how to clap this rhythm, we can write in the numbers underneath each bar to help us keep track of each main pulse beat. This is sometimes called 'counting the rhythm'.

When counting crotchets, use the number of the pulse beat. When counting quavers, add a '+' after the pulse beat, and when counting semiquavers, use 'e + a' after the main pulse beat.

Listen to this rhythm being performed with the counting. The rhythm is played through twice.

 1.08 Crotchet, Quaver, and Semiquaver Rhythm with Counting

 ## Spotlight: Percussion/Drum Clef

The rhythms above have two thick lines at the beginning – these lines are called a percussion/drum clef:

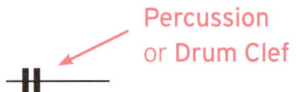

This clef is often used to write down music that doesn't have a specific pitch. We'll look at clefs in more detail in a later section.

 ## Extra Info: Rhythmic Awareness

It's important to have a strong rhythmic awareness and a good sense of time. The rhythmic reading and writing exercises in this section will help you develop these skills and will increase your rhythmic vocabulary.

Pulse and Rhythm

Exercises: Read the Rhythm (Part 1)

Try clapping the rhythms below which combine the three note values we have looked at so far – crotchets, quavers, and semiquavers. Before you begin, write in the numbers like in the previous example to help you keep track of each pulse beat.

Tap your foot on each pulse beat and then clap the rhythm over the top. Pick a tempo (BPM) that is comfortable for you. Once you have tried clapping the rhythm yourself, clap along with the recording to see if you were correct.

Next, try 'counting' the rhythm. Once you've mastered that, see if you can clap and count the rhythm at the same time. Listen to these rhythms being performed at 90 BPM. Each rhythm is played twice.

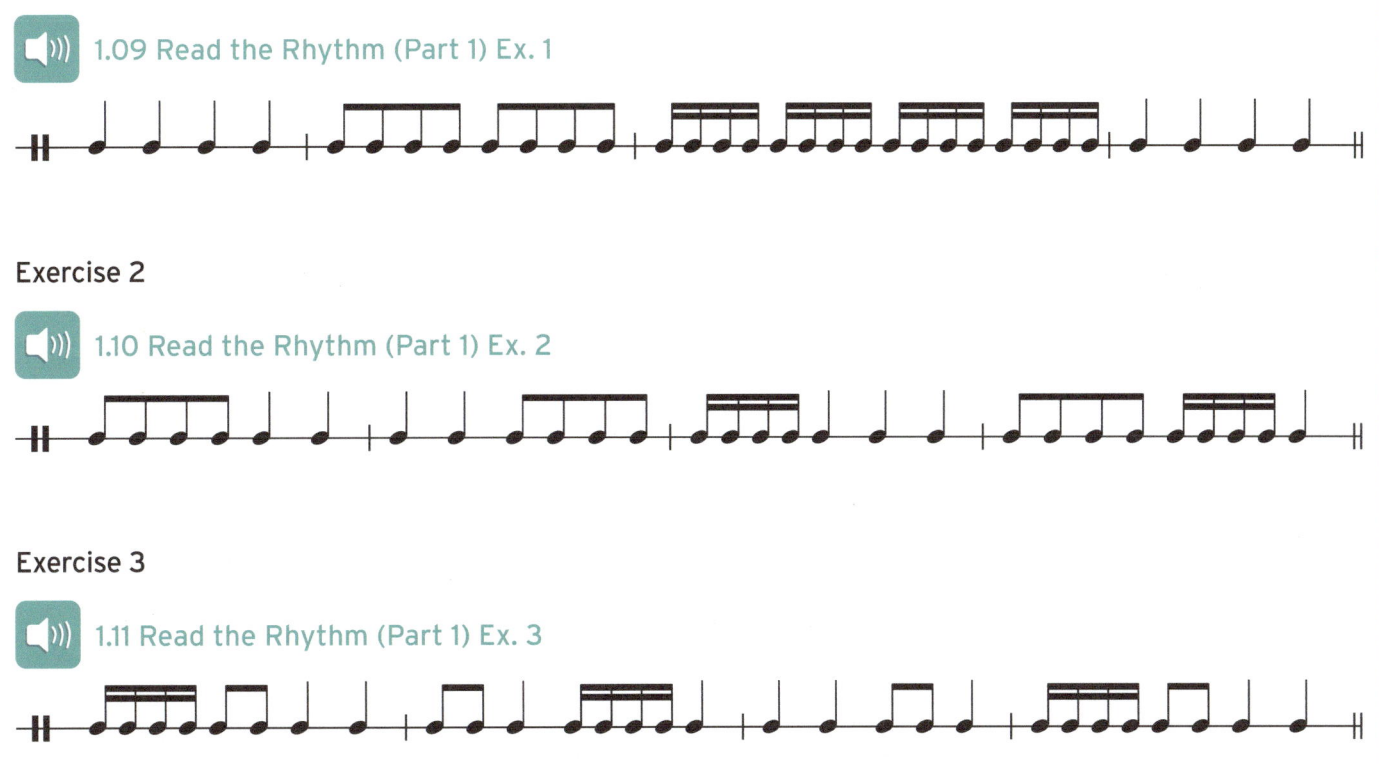

There are also note values that last longer than one pulse. A semibreve (or whole note) is held for four pulses. If a note is being held over several pulses, those numbers are put in brackets.

Here is one semibreve in the space of one bar:

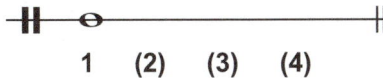

A minim (or half note) is held for two pulses.

Here are two minims in the space of one bar:

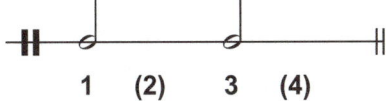

Exercises: Read the Rhythm (Part 2)

Try clapping the rhythms below which combine all the note values we have looked at so far – semibreves, minims, crotchets, quavers, and semiquavers. Before you begin, write in the numbers to help you keep track of each pulse beat.

Tap your foot on each pulse beat and then clap the rhythm over the top. Pick a tempo (BPM) that is comfortable for you. Once you have tried clapping the rhythm yourself, clap along and count the rhythm out loud with the track. Listen to these rhythms being performed at 90 BPM. Each rhythm is played twice.

Exercise 1

 1.12 Read the Rhythm (Part 2) Ex. 1

Exercise 2

 1.13 Read the Rhythm (Part 2) Ex. 2

Exercise 3

 1.14 Read the Rhythm (Part 2) Ex. 3

If you would like an additional challenge, try writing out your own 4-bar rhythms. You can use the blank manuscript paper at the back of this book to help you. Writing music by hand is a great way of becoming more familiar with how the notes look on paper!

Noteheads, Stems, Tails & Beams

To write down rhythms, we need to understand the various parts of a note. For example, this minim is made up of a stem and a notehead:

Notes with a stem can point upwards or downwards. When a stem points upwards, the stem should be on the right-hand side of the notehead, and when a note points downwards, the stem should be on the left-hand side of the notehead:

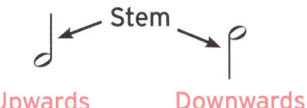

Upwards   Downwards

So far, all the semiquavers and quavers we have looked at have been linked together.

Group of 4 quavers   Group of 4 semiquavers

However, quavers and semiquavers can exist on their own. A single quaver consists of a notehead, a stem, and a tail:

Stem → ♪ ← Tail
       ← Notehead
Quaver

A single semiquaver is similar, however, there are two tails rather than one:

Stem → 𝅘𝅥𝅯 ← Tails
       ← Notehead
Semiquaver

If a note has a tail, then it is always drawn on the right-hand side of the stem whether the note is pointing upwards or downwards:

♪♩ ♪♩

Only notes with tails such as quavers and semiquavers can be linked together. They are connected by a line known as a beam. This process is called beaming and it makes notes much easier to read as you learn to recognise groups of notes, rather than each individual note value.

For example, four single quavers become beamed quavers:

Beam

The same applies to semiquavers, which have two tails and are connected by a double beam:

Double beam

There can also be different combinations of quavers and semiquavers within the same pulse. For example:

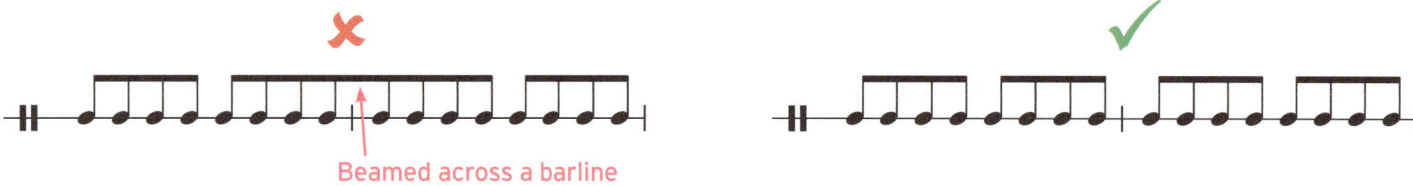

There are **three** rules to remember when beaming notes together. These help to make reading rhythms clearer, as it's easier to see where the notes fall in relation to the beats of the bar:

1. Do not beam across a barline.

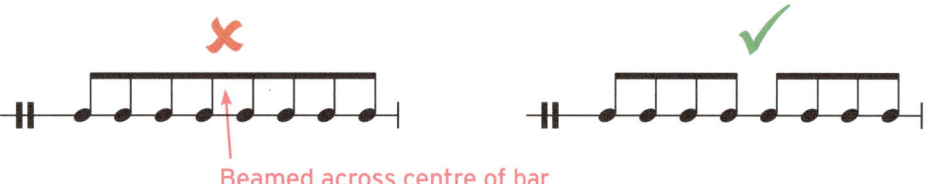

Beamed across a barline

2. Do not beam across the centre of the bar. For example, if there are four pulse beats in a bar there shouldn't be any beams between beats 2 and 3.

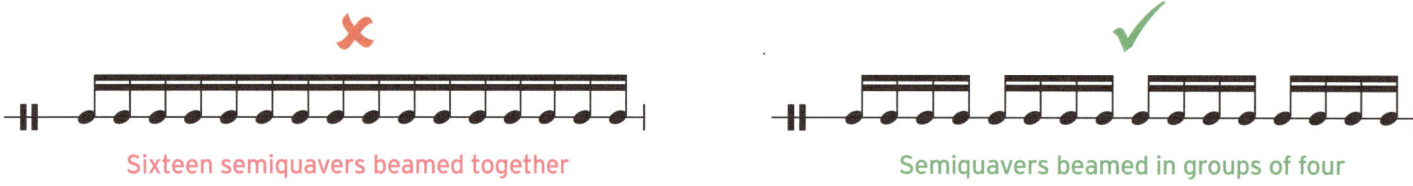

Beamed across centre of bar

3. A maximum of four semiquavers can be beamed together.

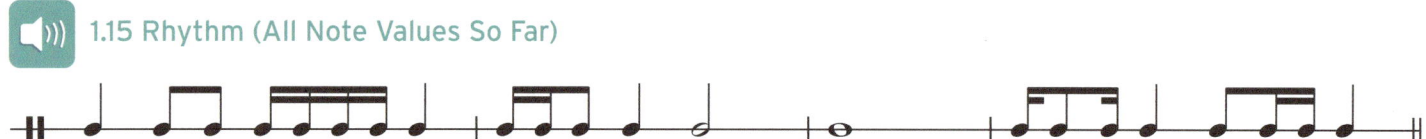

Sixteen semiquavers beamed together   Semiquavers beamed in groups of four

The following 4-bar rhythm contains all the note values we have encountered so far.

🔊 1.15 Rhythm (All Note Values So Far)

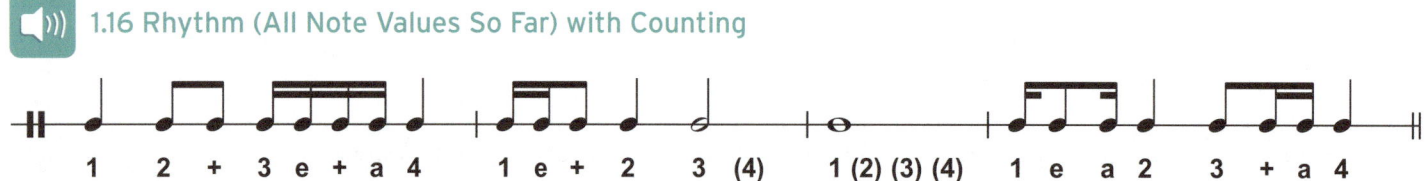

We can count the rhythm by writing in the numbers below. Listen to this rhythm being performed with the counting – the rhythm is played through twice.

🔊 1.16 Rhythm (All Note Values So Far) with Counting

1   2   +   3 e + a   4   1 e +   2   3   (4)   1 (2) (3) (4)   1   e   a   2   3   +   a   4

Pulse and Rhythm

Exercises: Read the Rhythm (Part 3)

Try clapping the rhythms below. Before you begin, write in the numbers to help you keep track of each pulse beat.

Tap your foot on each pulse beat and then clap the rhythm over the top. Pick a tempo (BPM) that is comfortable for you. Once you have tried clapping the rhythm yourself, clap along with the track. Try counting the rhythm out loud too. Listen to these rhythms being performed at 90 BPM. Each rhythm is played twice.

Exercise 1

 1.17 Read the Rhythm (Part 3) Ex. 1

Exercise 2

 1.18 Read the Rhythm (Part 3) Ex. 2

Exercise 3

 1.19 Read the Rhythm (Part 3) Ex. 3

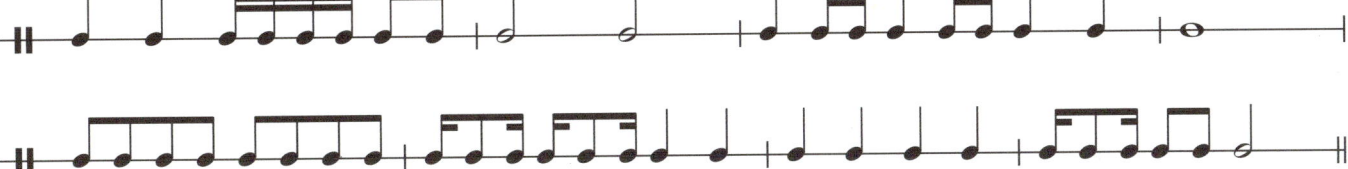

Exercise 4

 1.20 Read the Rhythm (Part 3) Ex. 4

Exercise: Transcribe the Rhythm

Listening, or 'aural' skills, are very important for musicians. Often, we need to be able to hear a musical phrase, sing or play it back, and then write it down. We call this process transcribing.

Listen to the tracks below and transcribe the rhythms – the first bar of each rhythm has been transcribed already. You'll hear a count-in ('1, 2, 3, 4') followed by the rhythm. Be aware that the rhythms are played at different tempos (BPMs). Each exercise will be played twice. Refer to the previous section on 'beaming' to make sure you are writing the rhythms correctly.

Helpful hint! Try learning and memorising the whole rhythm by ear before you begin writing it down.

Exercise 1 Crotchets and quavers

🔊 1.21 Transcribe the Rhythm Ex. 1

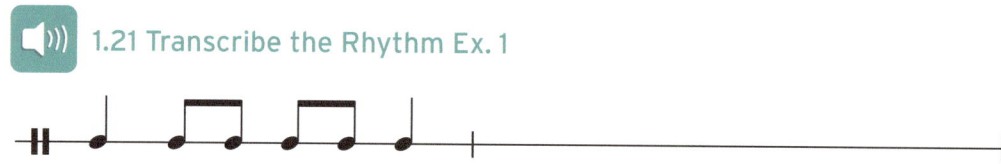

Exercise 2 Crotchets, quavers, and semiquavers

🔊 1.22 Transcribe the Rhythm Ex. 2

Exercise 3 Semibreves, minims, crotchets, and semiquavers

🔊 1.23 Transcribe the Rhythm Ex. 3

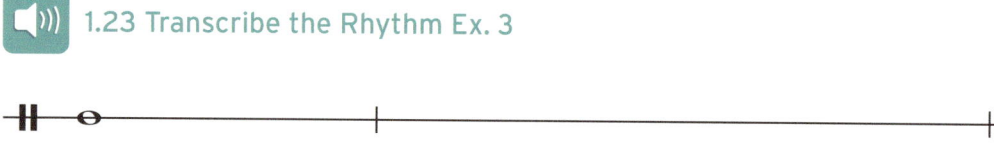

Pulse and Rhythm

Now try transcribing these 4-bar rhythms – two bars in each have been provided for you.

Exercise 4 Crotchets and quavers

🔊 1.24 Transcribe the Rhythm Ex. 4

Exercise 5 Crotchets, quavers, and semiquavers

🔊 1.25 Transcribe the Rhythm Ex. 5

Exercise 6 Minims, crotchets, quavers, and semiquavers

🔊 1.26 Transcribe the Rhythm Ex. 6

Transcribe the following rhythms. Here, the first bar has been provided for you.
Exercise 7

🔊 1.27 Transcribe the Rhythm Ex. 7

Exercise 8

🔊 1.28 Transcribe the Rhythm Ex. 8

Answers can be found online, see page 8 for details.

Summary: Note Pyramid

So far, we have looked at the most common note values – semibreve, minim, crotchet, quaver, and semiquaver. Here is a visual representation of how these common note values divide. This is sometimes called a note pyramid.

Semibreve / Whole Note
4 beats

Minim / Half Note
2 beats

Crotchet / Quarter Note
1 beat

Quaver / Eighth Note
½ beat

Semiquaver / 16th Note
¼ beat

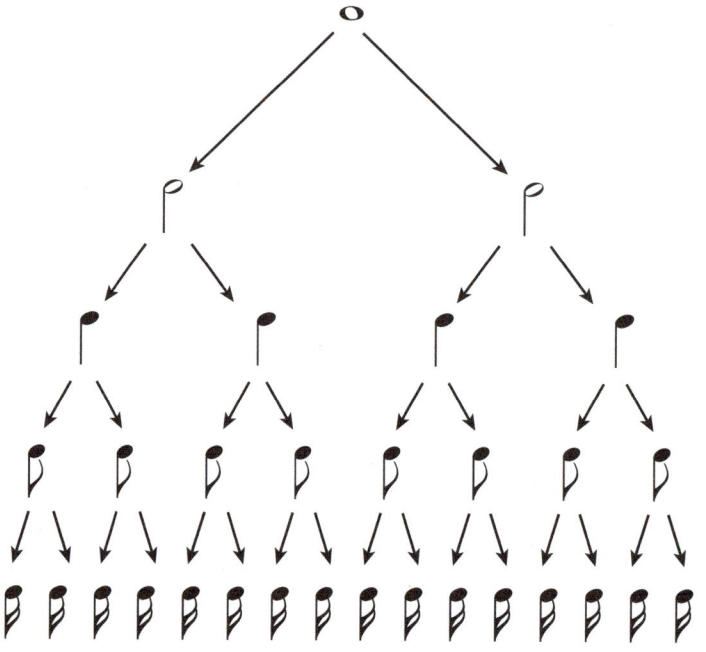

In other words, you can fit:

- Two minims in the space of one semibreve;
- Two crotchets in the space of one minim;
- Two quavers in the space of one crotchet;
- Two semiquavers in the space of one quaver.

Spotlight: Short Note Values

There are note values that are even shorter than semiquavers, however, they are quite rare – demisemiquavers and hemidemisemiquavers.

Pulse and Rhythm

 **Questions**

Here are some questions on the topics covered so far in this section.

1. What does **BPM** stand for? ....

2. True or False: **Tempo** means the speed of the music. ....

3. How many beat(s) is a **crotchet** worth? ....

4. How many beat(s) is a **minim** worth? ....

5. How many **minims** fit into the space of one **semibreve**? ....

6. What is another name for a **semiquaver**? ....

7. How many **quavers** fit into the space of one **crotchet**? ....

8. How many **semiquavers** fit into the space of one **crotchet**? ....

9. What separates each **bar**? ....

10. How many beats is a **semibreve** worth? ....

Answers can be found online, see page 8 for details.

Rests

When we want musicians to sing or play, we give them different kinds of musical notes. However, what do we use if we want there to be silence? This is called a rest.

Just like the symbols for the various note values, there are also symbols for the different types of rests.

A crotchet rest (or quarter-note rest) looks like this.
This means rest for one beat – the same length as a crotchet.

A quaver rest (or eighth-note rest) looks like this.
This means rest for half a beat – the same length as a quaver.

Extra Info: Musical Stave

Notice that these rests have been drawn on five lines, rather than one. These five lines together are called the musical stave. Don't worry about this for the moment, we will look at staves in more detail later.

Look at the 4-bar rhythm below which includes crotchet and quaver notes as well as crotchet and quaver rests. Listen to this rhythm being performed – played twice.

 1.29 4-Bar Rhythm (Crotchet and Quaver Notes and Rests)

Like before, we can count this rhythm using numbers. Listen to this rhythm being performed with the counting – played twice.

 1.30 4-Bar Rhythm (Crotchet and Quaver Notes and Rests) with Counting

Pulse and Rhythm

Exercises: Read the Rhythm (Part 4)

Try clapping the rhythms below which combine crotchet and quaver notes and rests. Before you begin, write in the numbers to help you keep track of each pulse beat. Rests sometimes cause musicians to rush ahead – make sure you keep a strong sense of pulse.

Tap your foot on each pulse beat and then clap the rhythm over the top. Pick a tempo (BPM) that is comfortable for you. Once you have tried clapping the rhythm yourself, clap along with the track. Listen to these tracks being performed at 90 BPM. Each track is played twice.

Exercise 1

 1.31 Read the Rhythm (Part 4) Ex. 1

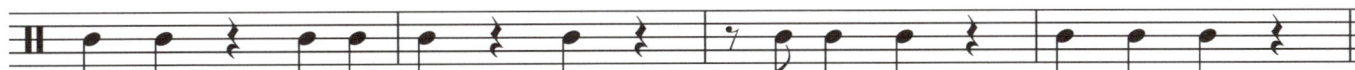

Exercise 2

 1.32 Read the Rhythm (Part 4) Ex. 2

Exercise 3

 1.33 Read the Rhythm (Part 4) Ex. 3

There are also rests that last longer than one beat.

This is a semibreve rest (or whole-note rest). This rest lasts four beats – the same length as a semibreve. This rest hangs from the fourth line up from the bottom. This is also known as a whole-bar rest.

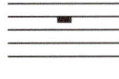

This is a minim rest (or half-note rest). This rest lasts for two beats – the same length as a minim. This rest sits on the third line from the bottom.

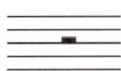

Look at the 4-bar rhythm below which includes semibreve and minim rests.
Listen to this rhythm being performed – played twice.

 1.34 4-Bar Rhythm (Semibreve and Minim Rests)

We can count the rhythm by writing in the numbers below. Notice that we count the silent beats too.
Listen to this rhythm being performed with the counting – played twice.

 1.35 4-Bar Rhythm (Semibreve and Minim Rests) with Counting

Exercise: Add the Rest

Go through the following rhythms – the rests are missing. **Add the rests in the gaps.** These could be either semibreve, minim, crotchet, or quaver rests. There should be **four pulses** in each bar.

Make sure the rests look like the examples from earlier in the section. Crotchet and quaver rests should sit vertically in the middle of the stave. Semibreve rests should hang from the fourth line up from the bottom. Minim rests should sit on the third line from the bottom.

Exercise 1

Exercise 2

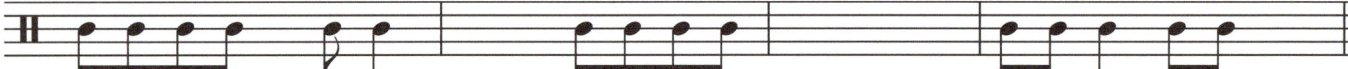

Exercise 3

Answers can be found online, see page 8 for details.

Pulse and Rhythm

A semiquaver rest lasts for a quarter of a beat – the same length as a semiquaver. The semiquaver rest sits vertically in the middle of the stave.

 **Spotlight: Semiquaver Rests**

It can sometimes be confusing to remember the difference between a quaver and semiquaver note or rest. Remember a quaver has one tail, a semiquaver has two tails.

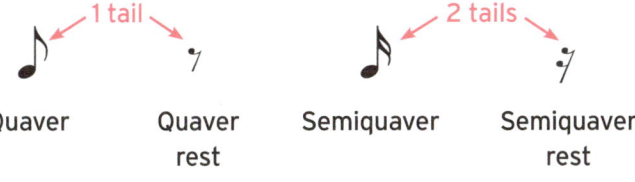

A semiquaver rest could appear anywhere within a group of four. Notice where there is a rest in the middle of a group, the beam can be written across it. This makes these types of rhythms easier to read as you can clearly see the four semiquavers as one group.

1st semiquaver   2nd semiquaver   3rd semiquaver   4th semiquaver

The following rhythm contains crotchets and semiquavers, with a semiquaver rest on the **first semiquaver** in every group of four. You will notice that the rhythm appears on different beats of the bar.

All the following examples are played twice.

 1.36 4-Bar Rhythm (Crotchets and Semiquaver Rests)

We can count the rhythm by writing in the numbers below.

 1.37 4-Bar Rhythm (Crotchets and Semiquaver Rests) with Counting

In the example below, the semiquaver rest is on the **second semiquaver** in every group of four.

 1.38 4-Bar Rhythm (2nd Semiquaver Rests)

We can count the rhythm by writing in the numbers below.

 1.39 4-Bar Rhythm (2nd Semiquaver Rests) with Counting

1 2 e + a 3 4   1 2 3 4 e + a   1 e + a 2 3 4   1 2 3 e + a 4

In the example below, the semiquaver rest is on the **third semiquaver** in every group of four.

 1.40 4-Bar Rhythm (3rd Semiquaver Rests)

We can count the rhythm by writing in the numbers below.

 1.41 4-Bar Rhythm (3rd Semiquaver Rests) with Counting

1 2 3 e + a 4   1 e + a 2 3 4   1 2 e + a 3 4   1 2 3 4 e + a

In this example, the semiquaver rest is on the **fourth semiquaver** in every group of four.

 1.42 4-Bar Rhythm (4th Semiquaver Rests)

Pulse and Rhythm

We can count the rhythm by writing in the numbers below.

 1.43 4-Bar Rhythm (4th Semiquaver Rests) with Counting

1   2 e + a 3   4   1   2   3 e + a 4   1 e + a 2   3   4   1   2   3   4 e + a

The 4-bar rhythm below includes semiquaver rests on every division of the beat.

 1.44 4-Bar Rhythm (Every Division Semiquaver Rests)

We can count the rhythm by writing in the numbers below.

 1.45 4-Bar Rhythm (Every Division Semiquaver Rests) with Counting

1   2 e + a 3   4   1 e + a 2 + 3   4   1 e + a 2 e + 3 (4)   1 e + a 2   3 + 4

Exercise: Creative Task - Rhythms

Write your own 4-bar rhythm using crotchets, quavers and semiquavers, include some rests. Make sure each bar adds up to 4 beats.

This is a creative exercise, so there are no 'answers'.

Exercises: Read the Rhythm (Part 5)

Try clapping the rhythms below. Before you begin, write in the numbers to help you keep track of each pulse beat.

Tap your foot on each pulse beat and then clap the rhythm over the top. Pick a tempo (BPM) that is comfortable for you. Once you have tried clapping the rhythm yourself, clap along with the track. Listen to these tracks being performed at 90 BPM. Each track is played twice.

Exercise 1

 1.46 Read the Rhythm (Part 5) Ex. 1

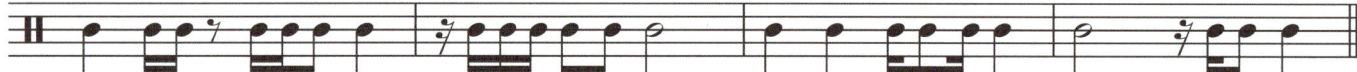

Exercise 2

 1.47 Read the Rhythm (Part 5) Ex. 2

Exercise 3

 1.48 Read the Rhythm (Part 5) Ex. 3

Exercise 4

 1.49 Read the Rhythm (Part 5) Ex. 4

Dots

Any note or rest can have a dot added to the right of it. When a dot is added, the note or rest becomes longer by half its value.

For example, if a minim has a dot next to it, it becomes the length of a minim and a crotchet joined together (eg three beats).

This is called a dotted minim.

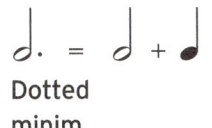

Dotted minim

If a crotchet has a dot next to it, it becomes the length of a crotchet and a quaver joined together (eg 1½ beats).

This is called a dotted crotchet.

Dotted crotchet

Look at the 4-bar rhythm below which features dotted minims and crotchets. Listen to this rhythm being performed – played twice.

 1.50 4-Bar Rhythm (Dotted Minims and Crotchets)

We can count the rhythm by writing in the numbers below. Listen to this rhythm being performed with the counting – played twice.

 1.51 4-Bar Rhythm (Dotted Minims and Crotchets) with Counting

1   (2)   +   3   (4)   1   (2)   (3)   4   +   1   2   3   (4)   +   1   (2)   (3)   4

Exercises: Read the Rhythm (Part 6)

Try clapping the rhythms below which include dotted minims and dotted crotchets. Before you begin, write in the numbers to help you keep track of each pulse beat.

Tap your foot on each pulse beat and then clap the rhythm over the top. Pick a tempo (BPM) that is comfortable for you. Once you have tried clapping the rhythm yourself, clap along with the track. Listen to these tracks being performed at 90 BPM. Each track is played twice.

Exercise 1

 1.52 Read the Rhythm (Part 6) Ex. 1

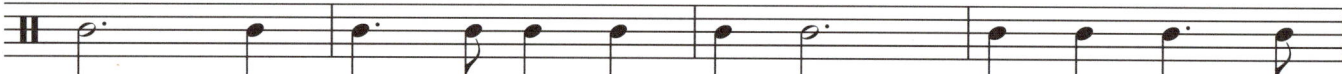

Exercise 2

 1.53 Read the Rhythm (Part 6) Ex. 2

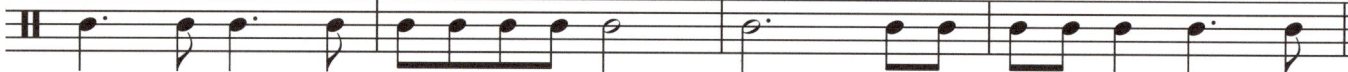

Exercise 3

 1.54 Read the Rhythm (Part 6) Ex. 3

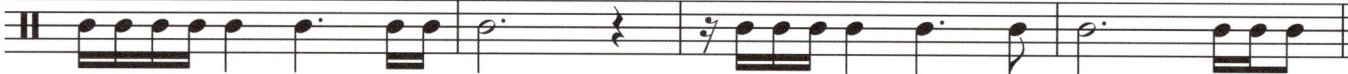

Exercise 4

 1.55 Read the Rhythm (Part 6) Ex. 4

Pulse and Rhythm

If a quaver has a dot next to it, it becomes the length of a quaver and a semiquaver joined together (eg ¾ of a beat).

This is called a .

Dotted quaver

Look at the 4-bar rhythm below which includes dotted notes. Listen to this rhythm being performed – played twice.

🔊 1.56 4-Bar Rhythm (Dotted Notes)

We can count the rhythm by writing in the numbers below. Listen to this rhythm being performed with the counting – played twice.

🔊 1.57 4-Bar Rhythm (Dotted Notes) with Counting

 1 (2) + 3 e + 4(e+)a   1 (2) (3)   4   1   +   2   +   a 3(e+)a 4   +   1 (2) + 3 (4)

 **Extra Info: Dotted Rests**

Rests can also be dotted, and the same principle applies.

Exercises: Read the Rhythm (Part 7)

Try clapping the rhythms below. Before you begin, write in the numbers to help you keep track of each pulse beat.

Tap your foot on each pulse beat and then clap the rhythm over the top. Pick a tempo (BPM) that is comfortable for you. Once you have tried clapping the rhythm yourself, clap along with the track. Listen to these tracks being performed at 90 BPM. Each track is played twice.

Exercise 1

 1.58 Read the Rhythm (Part 7) Ex. 1

Exercise 2

 1.59 Read the Rhythm (Part 7) Ex. 2

Exercise 3

 1.60 Read the Rhythm (Part 7) Ex. 3

Exercise 4

 1.61 Read the Rhythm (Part 7) Ex. 4

Ties

Ties are curved lines that join notes together – they are played as if they are one note. Ties are used to extend the length of a note. For example, ties can be used to hold notes over a barline:

Here, a crotchet (one beat) is tied to a dotted minim (three beats), meaning that in total the note is held for four beats.

Extra Info: Ties

It's important to remember that ties can only be used to tie together notes of the same pitch. We'll look at pitch in more detail in the next section.

Ties can also be used within a bar, however, they should only be written when there isn't a longer note value that can be used instead. For example, look at the following bars in the left column and see the correct notation in the right column. In the right column, the rhythms are much easier to read as they use notes of a longer value, rather than ties.

Spotlight

Only notes can be tied together. Rests cannot be tied.

Exercises: Read the Rhythm (Part 8)

Try clapping the rhythms below. Before you begin, write in the numbers to help you keep track of each pulse beat.

Tap your foot on each pulse beat and then clap the rhythm over the top. Pick a tempo (BPM) that is comfortable for you. Once you have tried clapping the rhythm yourself, clap along with the track. Listen to these tracks being performed at 90 BPM. Each track is played twice.

Exercise 1

 1.62 Read the Rhythm (Part 8) Ex. 1

Exercise 2

 1.63 Read the Rhythm (Part 8) Ex. 2

Exercise 3

 1.64 Read the Rhythm (Part 8) Ex. 3

Exercise 4

 1.65 Read the Rhythm (Part 8) Ex. 4

Pulse and Rhythm

Summary: Rests

A rest is a musical symbol that represents the silence between notes. As a reminder, the diagram below shows the rests we have looked at so far, with their equivalent note value.

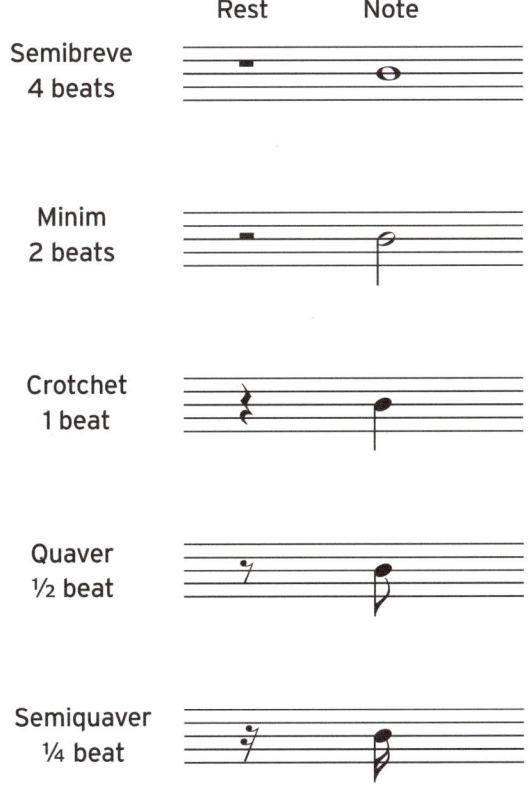

If a note is dotted, then the note or rest becomes longer by half its value. Ties are used to extend the length of a note when writing a single note of a longer value isn't possible.

Familiarise yourself with this rhythmic terminology. It can be a lot to learn at first, but longer term, increasing your awareness of these concepts will help improve your rhythmic vocabulary and help you articulate various grooves and feels when working with other musicians in a band.

For example, the drummer might be playing semiquavers (16th notes) on the hi-hat, but you might suggest that quavers (eighth notes) are more appropriate. Being able to use specific terminology will help your communication with other musicians when performing or writing music together.

Time Signatures

A time signature tells us how many pulse beats are in a bar. A time signature usually appears at the beginning of a piece of music and consists of two numbers stacked on top of one another. The top number tells us how many pulse beats are in each bar.

Up until now, we have only looked at examples that have four pulse beats in every bar. However, there are other time signatures that appear in popular music.

$\frac{2}{4}$ $\frac{3}{4}$ $\frac{4}{4}$

2 beats per bar   3 beats per bar   4 beats per bar

The bottom number of the time signature indicates what kind of beats these are, whether they are minim, crotchet, or quaver pulse beats.

If the bottom number is a four, this means that these are crotchet pulse beats. A crotchet is worth one beat so:

- a $\frac{2}{4}$ time signature means that there are two crotchet beats per bar;
- a $\frac{3}{4}$ time signature means that there are three crotchet beats per bar;
- a $\frac{4}{4}$ time signature means that there are four crotchet beats per bar;
- a $\frac{5}{4}$ time signature means that there are five crotchet beats per bar;
- and so on...

In the example below, we can see that there is a time signature of $\frac{3}{4}$. This means that all the note values and rests combined need to add up to **three** crotchet beats in each bar. After every three crotchet beats, we need to add a **barline**.

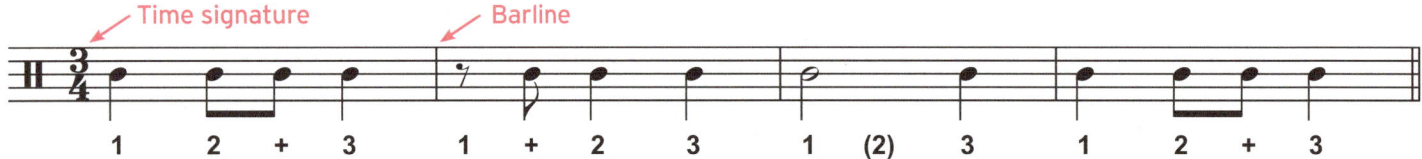

Any time signatures that have a 2, 3 or 4 at the top are known as simple time signatures. In simple time every beat can be divided in two – for example, a crotchet could be divided into two quavers.

Here's another example which has a time signature of $\frac{2}{4}$. This means that all the note values and rests need to add up to **two** crotchet beats in each bar. After every second crotchet beat, we need to add a **barline**.

Pulse and Rhythm

Exercises: Add the Barlines (Part 1)

Add barlines to the rhythms below. Remember to look at the time signature before you begin.

Example
Here the time signature is 4/4. We know this means that in each bar, all the note values and rests should add up to four crotchet beats.

Write in the numbers below each main pulse beat then add a barline after every four crotchet beats.

1   2 e + a 3   +   4   1 + 2   3 + 4   1 (2) 3   4   1   2 + 3   4

Add barlines to every exercise, don't forget to add one at the end of each example.

Exercise 1

Exercise 2

Exercise 3

Exercise 4 Slightly trickier! 5/4 is an irregular time signature.

Answers can be found online, see page 8 for details.

Time Signatures

The time signature used in a piece of music can change the way it 'feels', so it's important to be able to recognise them. Use the following Spotify playlists to help you understand what these time signatures sound like when used in context. The more you listen to songs in these different time signatures, the more you'll learn what they sound like, and you'll begin to recognise them in the music you are listening to.

When listening to each track in the playlist, count along with the main beats.

Playlist: 4/4 Time Signatures

4/4 is by far the most widely used time signature in popular music. The playlist below is just a small selection of songs from a variety of genres.

- Joan Jett & the Blackhearts: I Love Rock 'N Roll
- Eurythmics, Annie Lennox, Dave Stewart: Sweet Dreams (Are Made of This)
- Queen: Don't Stop Me Now
- Madonna: Hung Up
- Whitney Houston: How Will I Know
- Jill Scott: Do You Remember
- Soul II Soul, Caron Wheeler: Keep On Movin'
- AC/DC: Highway to Hell
- Aerosmith: Walk This Way
- CHIC: Good Times
- John Denver: Take Me Home, Country Roads
- Disclosure, RAYE: Waterfall
- Elton John: I'm Still Standing
- George Ezra: Green Green Grass
- Coldplay: Yellow
- Led Zeppelin: Kashmir
- Shea Diamond: I Am America

Playlist: 3/4 Time Signatures

3/4 is another common time signature used in popular music. Sometimes it is referred to as a 'waltz' rhythm, although this terminology is used more in the context of classical music.

- Billie Marten: Cursive
- Bob Dylan: The Times They Are A-Changin'
- Lionel Richie: Three Times A Lady
- Jimi Hendrix: Manic Depression
- Billie Eilish: When the Party's Over
- Lizzy McAlpine: Where Do I Go?

Playlist: 2/4 Time Signatures

2/4 is rarely used in popular music and sounds very similar to 4/4 (two bars of 2/4 sound the same as one bar of 4/4). 2/4 has a 'march-like' quality and lends itself to more classical styles.

An example of 2/4 in a well-known context would be 'Zorba's Dance' by Mikis Theodorakis, which can be heard on the *Lock Stock & Two Smoking Barrels* soundtrack.

- Mikis Theodorakis: Zorba the Greek: Zorba's Dance
- Wolfgang Amadeus Mozart, Boris Apostolov: Turkish March
- Scott Joplin, Morten Gunnar Larsen: The Entertainer
- Pyotr Ilyich Tchaikovsky, Lior Rosner, Scott Dunn, Royal Philharmonic Orchestra: Dance of the Sugar Plum Fairy
- Frankie Yankovic And His Yanks: Beer Barrel Polka

Pulse and Rhythm

Exercise: What's the Time Signature?

Listen to the following tracks and work out whether the time signature is $\frac{4}{4}$ or $\frac{3}{4}$.

🔊 1.66 What's the Time Signature? Ex. 1 ....

🔊 1.67 What's the Time Signature? Ex. 2 ....

🔊 1.68 What's the Time Signature? Ex. 3 ....

Answers can be found online, see page 8 for details.

Summary

The 'time signature' of a piece of music tells you how many beats there are in a bar, and what kind of beats they are. Time signatures can change the way a piece of music 'feels' rhythmically.

In written music, time signatures usually appear at the beginning of a passage – the top number tells you how many beats are in each bar and the bottom number tells you what kind of note value those beats are.

Musical Building Blocks

In this section, we're going to look at the concept of 'pitch', and how pitches can be organised and written down. Pitches are more commonly known as 'notes'. Understanding how notes relate to one another allows you to experiment with melodies and chords.

We're going to look at how pitches can be written down; this is often called notation. Music notation is a fundamental tool for creating, communicating, and studying music. Developing your aural skills is crucial. It's the ability to notate specific chords, melodies, and voicings. It also allows you to interpret, reproduce, and analyse music more effectively, and it opens up other musical avenues for exploration.

The Musical Alphabet

When you sing or play, a soundwave is produced. A soundwave is a vibration of air particles which travel from the source of the sound to your ears.

All soundwaves travel at the same speed (340m/s) in air. However, the length of the soundwave (wavelength) and the frequency determine how high or low that sound is.

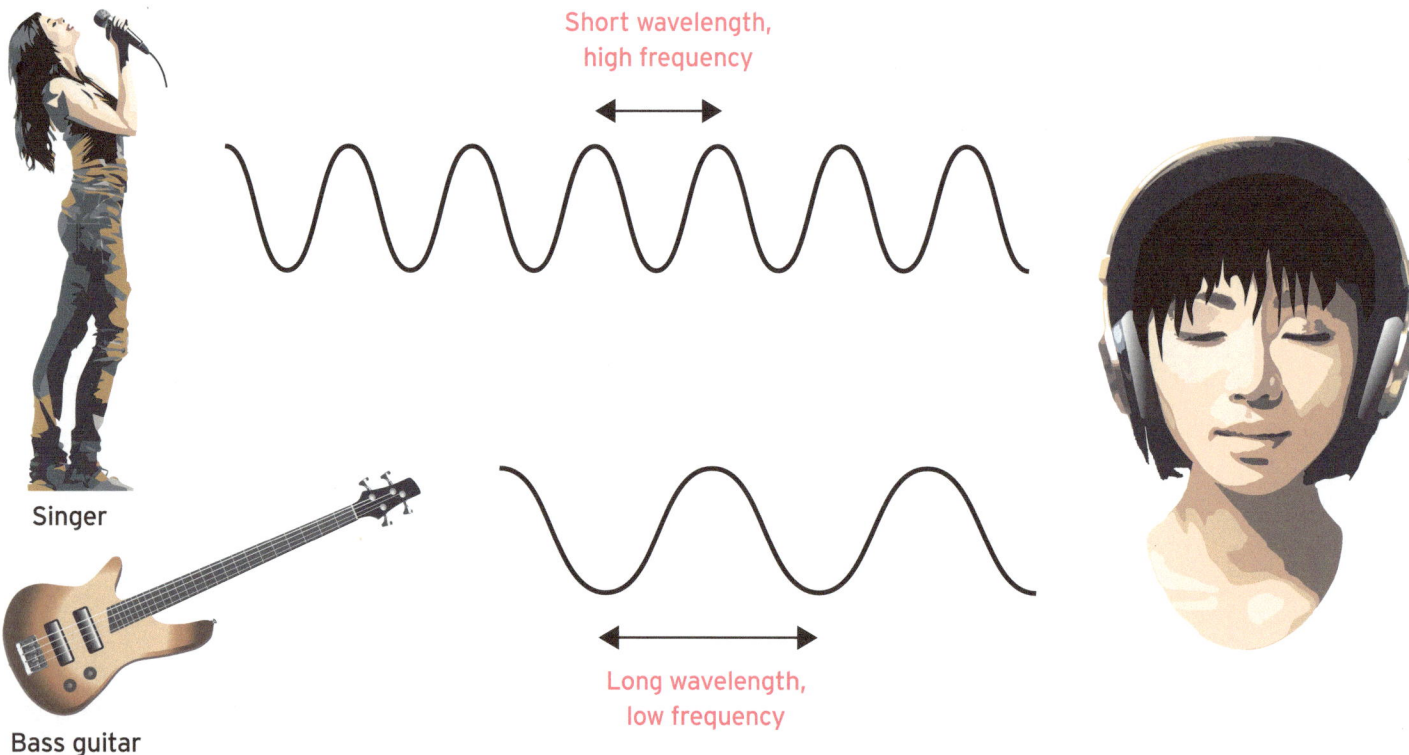

Pitch is essentially how high or low a sound is. In the above example, the singer is performing at the top of her vocal range, producing a high frequency and therefore a high pitch. The bass guitar has a lower frequency and therefore a lower pitch.

Musical Building Blocks

In most Western music, these pitches have been standardised and are known as notes. They are named after the first seven letters of the alphabet.

A B C D E F G

Below, these letters have been mapped onto the white keys on the piano, a really useful visual tool. As you move further up the piano to the right, the notes get higher in pitch.

Rather than continuing all the way through the alphabet as the notes get higher, once you reach G, you start the whole sequence again.

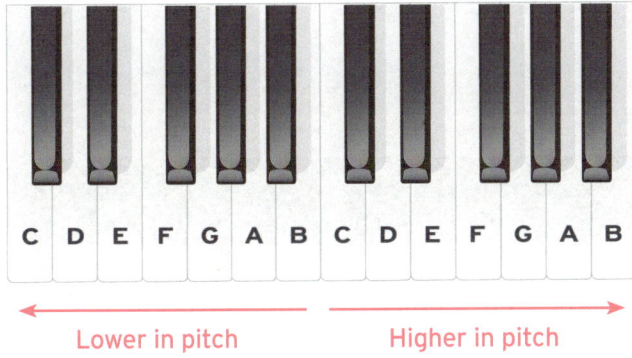

The distance between two notes with the same name, for example C to C, is called an octave.
An octave is a type of interval. We will look at intervals in more detail later.

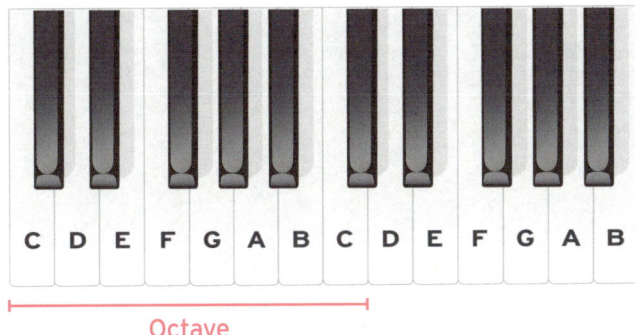

The electric guitar, acoustic guitar, and bass guitar work in a similar way – as you move further up the neck of the guitar along each string, the notes get higher in pitch.

 **Extra Info**

While you may not consider yourself a keyboard player, it is useful to have a working knowledge of the piano keyboard. It is a helpful visual representation of the notes available to us and will help to reinforce many of the topics covered in this book. There is a piano keyboard diagram in the Appendix section.

Understanding the layout of the keyboard is also beneficial if you are interested in music production as many Digital Audio Workstations (DAWs) use 'piano roll' for inputting and editing MIDI data.

The Stave

One way of notating music is to use these five horizontal lines, known as the musical *stave*.

Notes can either be placed on the lines or in the spaces in between.

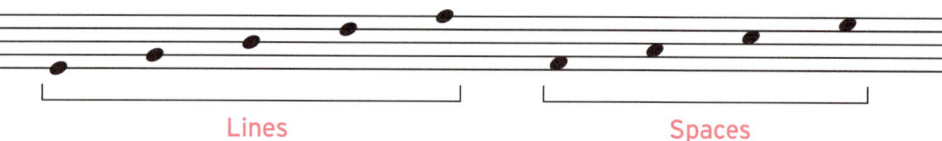

Lines   Spaces

 **Spotlight**

While notes can appear on any line or space, rests are always placed in the same place, vertically in the middle of the stave.

If you move up the piano the pitches get higher. This is the same on the stave – the higher the note on the stave, the higher the pitch. The lower the note on the stave, the lower the pitch.

Higher ↑   ↓ Lower

Musical Building Blocks

Clefs

To understand which note corresponds with which line or space, we need to use a clef. There are many clefs used in music, and the notes on the lines and spaces are different depending on which clef is being used. The four most used clefs in popular music are shown below.

Treble clef   Bass clef   Drum clef   TAB

As musicians, it's important to understand how all these clefs work, even though they may not be the clefs you use for the instrument you play. We will look at these clefs in more detail later but, for now, we will start with the treble clef.

The Treble Clef

The treble clef is the most common and is used by the vast majority of instruments. For example:

- the electric/acoustic guitar;
- the right hand of the piano;
- the trumpet;
- the saxophone;
- singers with higher voices (soprano or alto).

Sometimes the treble clef is known as the 'G clef' because the little loop in the centre of the clef wraps around the second line from the bottom, which is the note G.

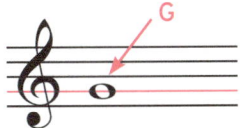

Once we know where G is placed on the stave we can easily work out the rest of the notes on the stave as they follow the sequence of the letters A-G.

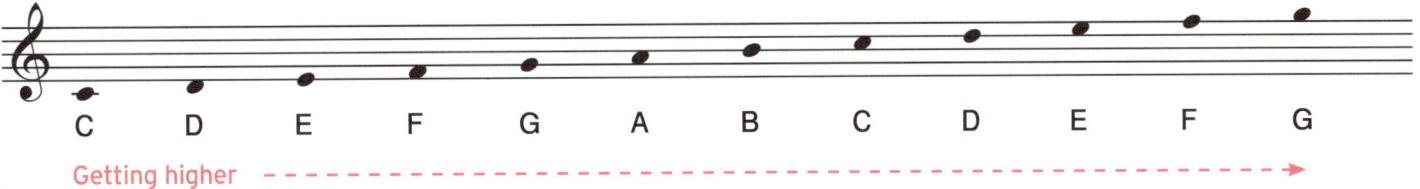

C   D   E   F   G   A   B   C   D   E   F   G

Getting higher - →

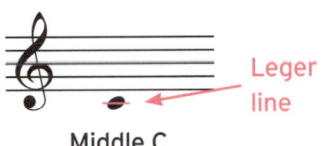

Middle C

Notice how the first C on the stave has a small line through it; we call this a leger line (also ledger line) and this helps us to read notes that are above or below the stave. This particular C is known as middle C or C4 (the fourth C that appears on a full-size, 88-key piano). This is usually the C closest to the middle of the piano.

These treble clef notes can be mapped onto the piano keyboard as seen below:

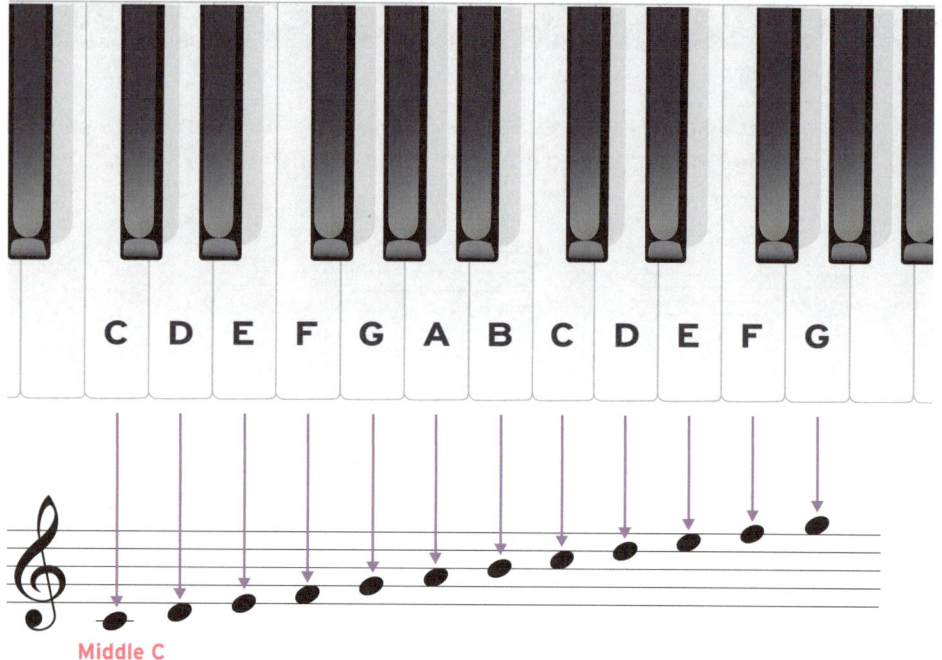

Middle C

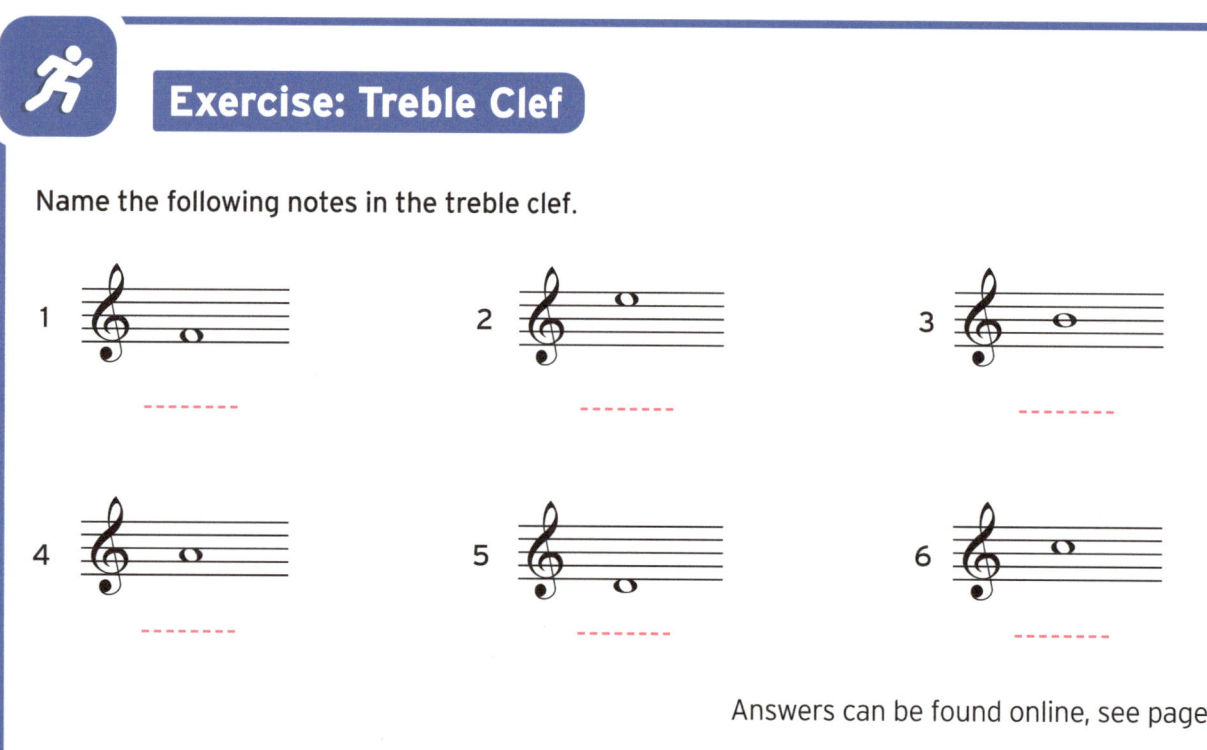

Exercise: Treble Clef

Name the following notes in the treble clef.

1.
2.
3.
4.
5.
6.

Answers can be found online, see page 8 for details.

Musical Building Blocks

The Bass Clef

The bass clef (as the name suggests) is used for instruments that have a lower pitch. For example:

- the bass guitar;
- the left hand of the piano;
- the trombone;
- singers with lower voices (eg, baritone or bass).

Sometimes the bass clef is known as the 'F clef' because the little loop at the top of the clef wraps around the second line from the top, which is the note F.

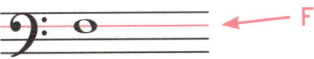

Once we know where F is placed on the stave we can easily work out the rest of the notes.

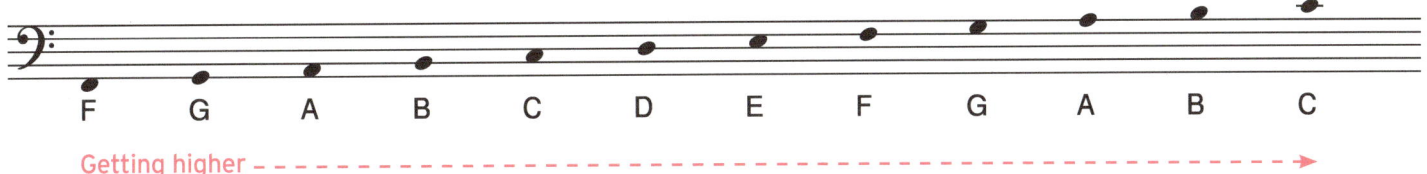

Getting higher ───▶

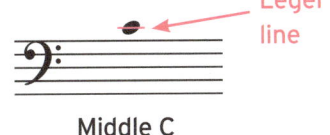

Middle C

Leger line — Middle C, or C4 also appears in the bass clef on the first leger line above the stave.

 **Extra Info**

Notice that middle C in the bass clef is the same as the treble clef but turned upside down.

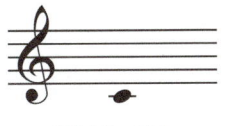 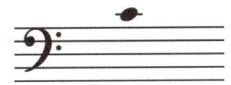

Middle C in the treble clef   Middle C in the bass clef

These bass clef notes can be mapped onto the piano keyboard as seen below:

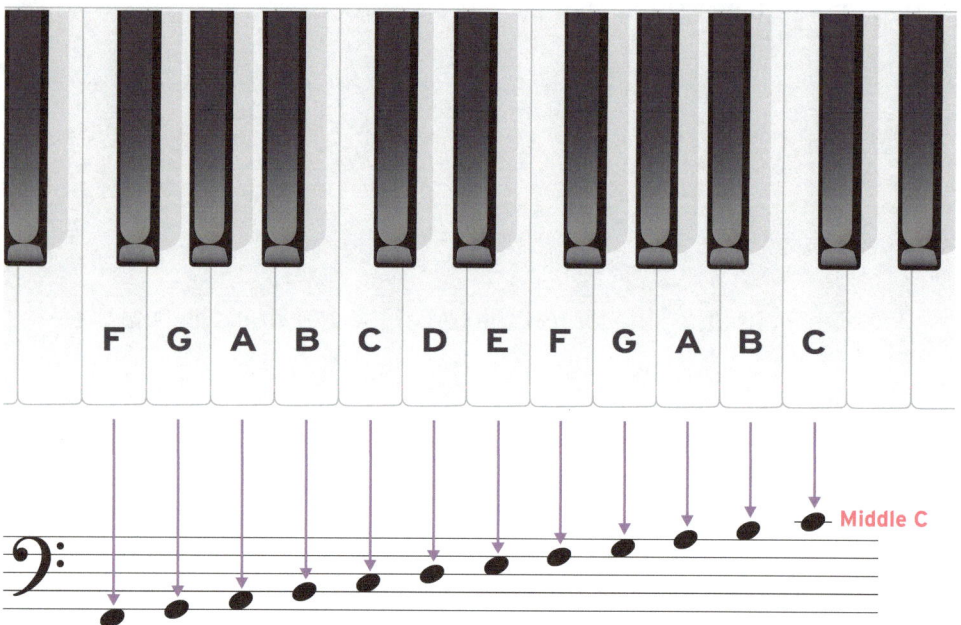

Exercise: Bass Clef

Name the following notes in the bass clef.

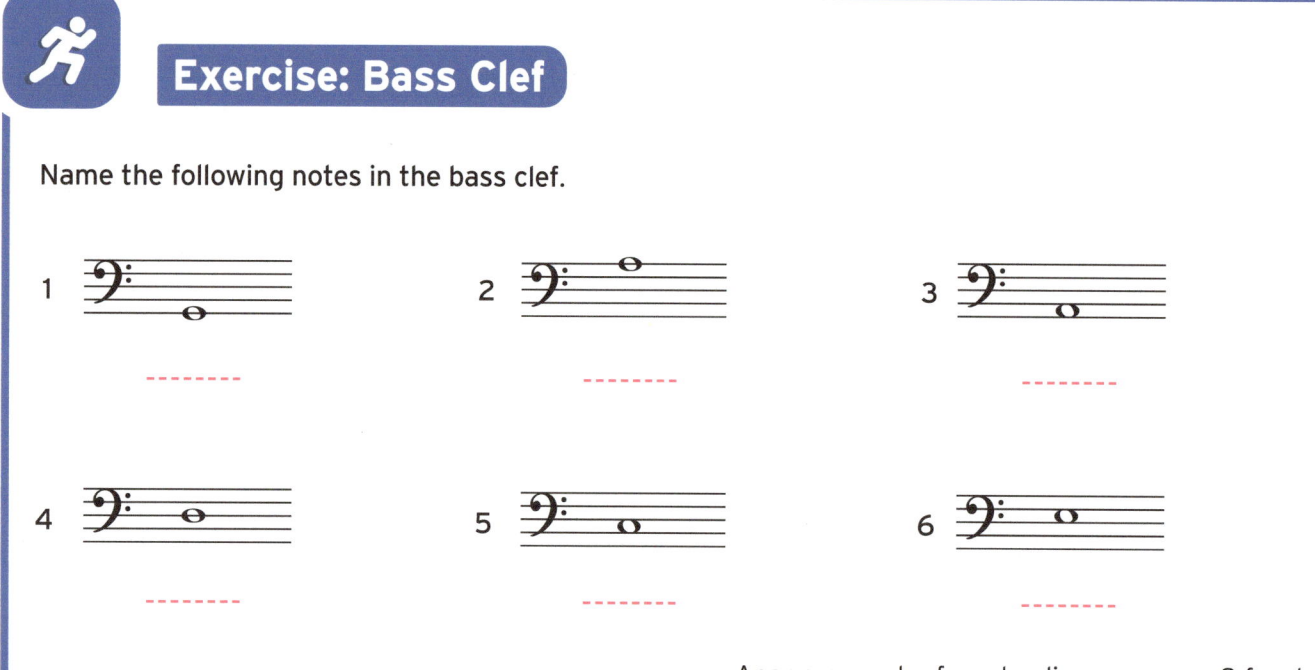

Answers can be found online, see page 8 for details.

Musical Building Blocks

The majority of the keyboard can then be mapped onto the treble and bass clefs, with the lower notes using the bass clef, and the higher notes using the treble clef.

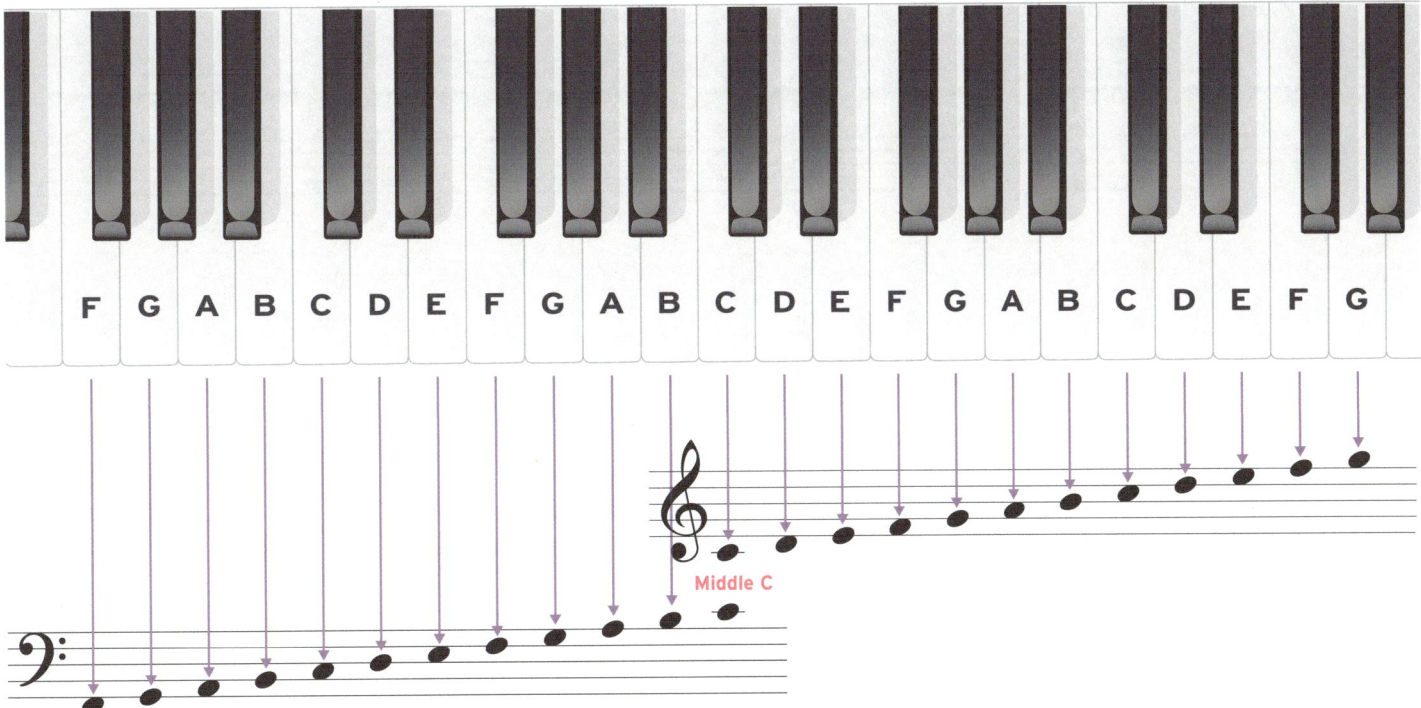

It isn't always practical to keep switching clefs, especially if just one note in the melody or chord goes above or below the stave. Therefore, leger lines can be used to add additional notes that go beyond the stave. For example:

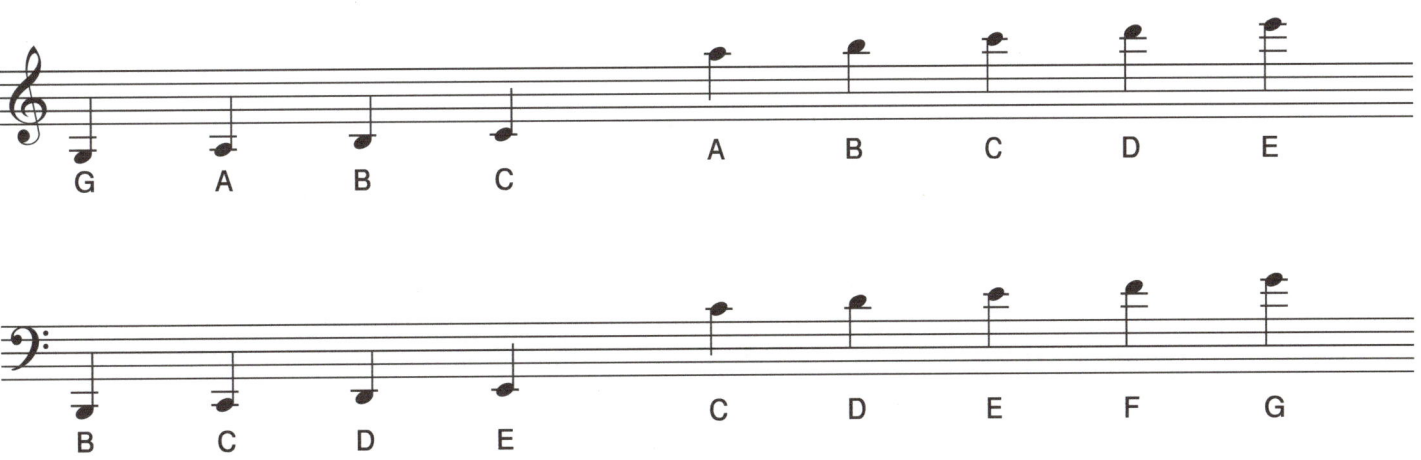

Drum Clef

Drum parts are notated using the drum clef which consists of two short vertical lines at the beginning of the stave. All drums are notated on the same stave:

Listen to this track which demonstrates the above drum groove.

 2.01 Drum Groove at 105 BPM

The kick drum sits in the first space, with the stems pointing downwards. The snare drum is notated in the space above the middle line, again with the stem pointing downwards and the hi-hat sits on top of the stave and uses a cross-notehead when played with a stick.

Tablature

Although guitar (electric and/or acoustic) notation can use the treble clef, some players prefer to use tablature (TAB) as a way of reading music.

There are six strings on the electric or acoustic guitar. From lowest to highest, these strings are tuned to E, A, D, G, B, and E (there are two E strings, two octaves apart). Standard guitar tab uses six horizontal lines with each one representing a different string.

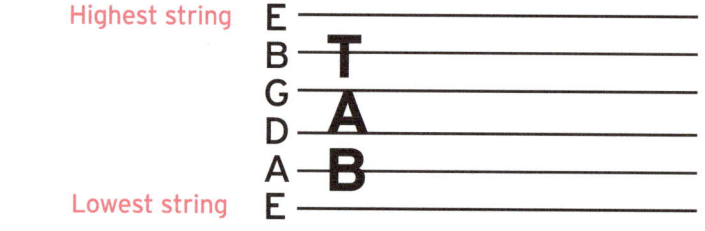

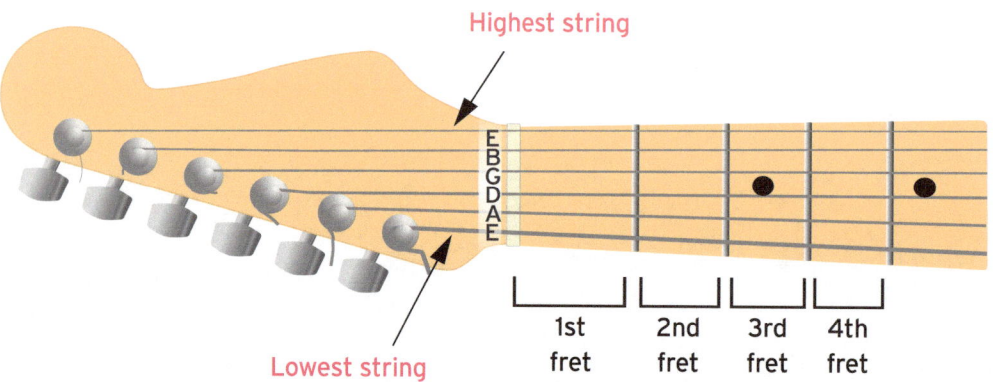

Musical Building Blocks   49

Guitar tab is read as if you're looking down at the guitar whilst playing. The numbers written under each rhythm, represent the fret of the guitar. The frets are numbered and span the whole of the neck of the guitar. The frets go up in semitones (or half steps) A semitone is the smallest distance between one note and another, we'll explore semitones more fully later.

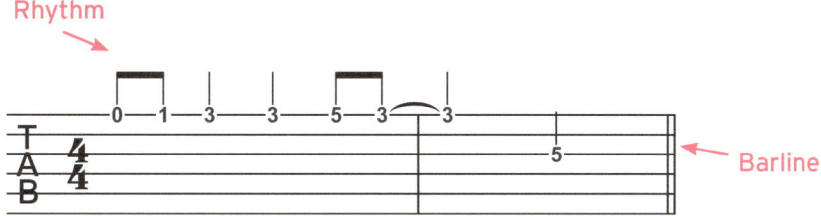

In these two bars, the first bar is written on the highest string (the E string). The first note has a '0' which means it is an open string; this makes the first note an E. The next note has a '1' so this note is played on the 1st fret which is an F, and so on. The '5' in the second bar is written on a different horizontal line – the G string. The 5th fret on the G string is a C.

If this melody was written using treble clef, it would look like this:

Bass tab (for bass guitars) works in the same way, except the bass guitar has four strings – E, A, D, and G (some bass guitars have five strings). Bass guitarists can also read using the bass clef.

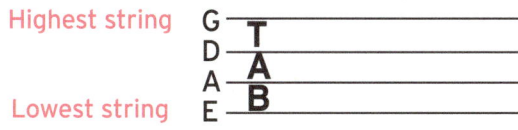

 **Extra Info**

While you may not be a guitarist, or need to be able to read TAB fluently, it's important to understand the different ways music can be written down and learnt.

In this book, we will mostly focus on the treble and bass clefs, however many guitarists (electric, acoustic, and bass) begin learning using TAB, so it's useful to understand the principles of how it works.

Sharps, Flats, and Naturals

So far, we have looked at the white keys on the piano which are named after the first seven letters of the alphabet: A, B, C, D, E, F, and G.

A note that has no sharp or flat is natural (♮). Therefore, all the white keys on the piano can be referred to as naturals. For example, C natural or D natural. However, you don't always have to say the word 'natural' – it's often assumed unless stated otherwise.

However, in Western music, there are twelve notes within each octave, and these remaining five notes are found on the black keys.

The black key directly to the right of a white key is known as a sharp (♯) and the black key to the left is a flat (♭). Each black key can be referred to by two names. For example, the black note directly to the right of C could be labelled C♯ or D♭ because it is also directly to the left of D.

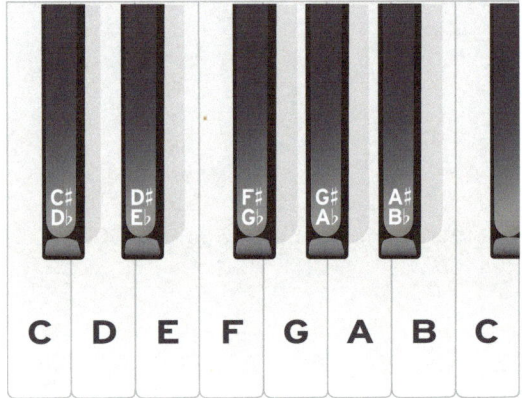

When all of these pitches are played in ascending or descending order we call it a chromatic scale. The term chromatic comes from a Greek word meaning 'all the colours'.

Listen to this track which demonstrates a chromatic scale from C played on the piano, ascending then descending.

 2.02 Chromatic Scale on Piano

To make a note sharp, it is raised by a semitone (or half step) and to make a note flat, it's lowered by a semitone. A semitone is the distance between one note and its next nearest note (either black or white) on either side. We'll look at semitones in more detail in the next section.

When writing sharps or flats on the stave, we place the sharp (♯) or flat (♭) to the left of the notehead. However, when saying the note name or writing it down as text, the accidental is after the note name, eg, C♯ or D♭.

 **Spotlight**

Sharp, flat, or natural symbols are sometimes referred to as 'accidentals' – that doesn't mean that they were a mistake! It's another term used for a sharp, flat, or natural, eg, 'there are lots of accidentals in this melody'.

Musical Building Blocks

Enharmonic Equivalents

Notes that have the same name (eg, C♯ and D♭) are called enharmonic equivalents and whether you 'spell' a note as a sharp or flat depends on the context. However, they sound the same, no matter whether they are labelled sharp or flat.

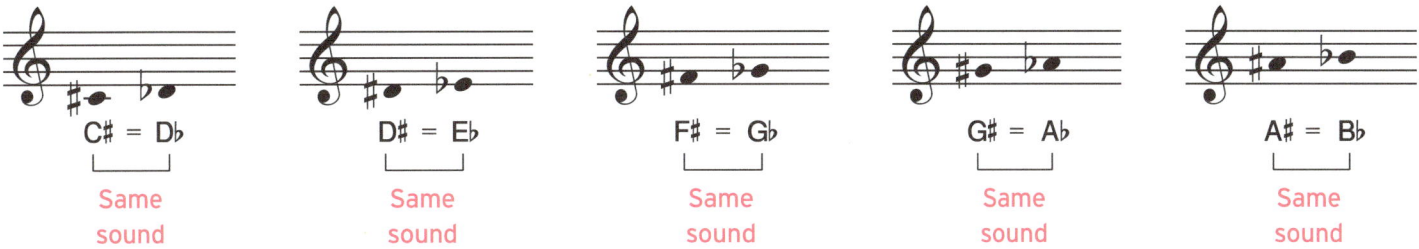

If a note in a bar has been made sharp or flat, this continues until the end of that bar. A natural sign can therefore also be used to cancel any previous sharps or flats.

For example, the melody below begins on an F♯ and there is another F♯ straight after – this doesn't need an accidental as the F remains sharp for the whole bar. In the third bar, there is an F♯ followed by an F natural, and a natural sign has been placed next to the note so the musician knows that it is no longer an F♯.

Exercise: Accidentals

Name the following notes. Make sure you take into account whether the notes are written in the treble or the bass clef.

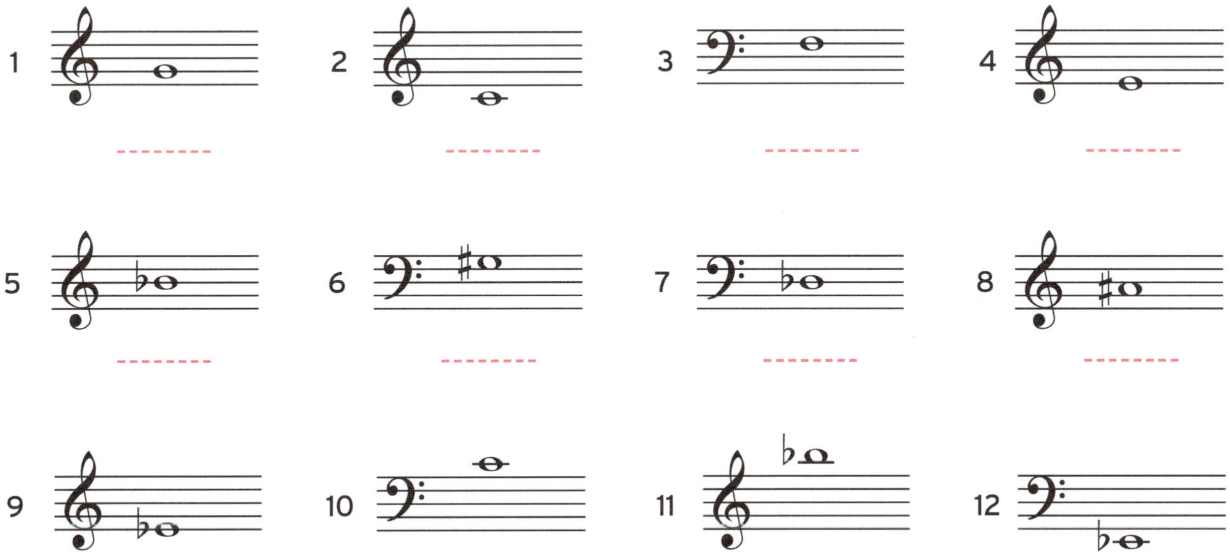

Answers can be found online, see page 8 for details.

You may have noticed there are no black notes between E and F, and B and C. This means that E and F, and B and C are a semitone (or half step) apart.

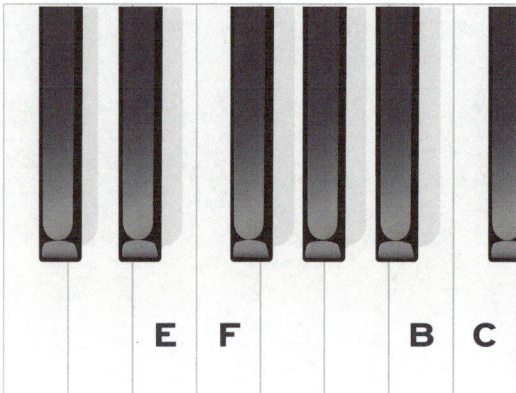

 **Extra Info**

In some circumstances, it is possible to refer to white keys as sharps or flats. For example, F♭ would be the same pitch as E natural, and C♭ would be the same pitch as B natural.

The following are all enharmonic equivalents – this means they have the same sound but can be spelt differently.

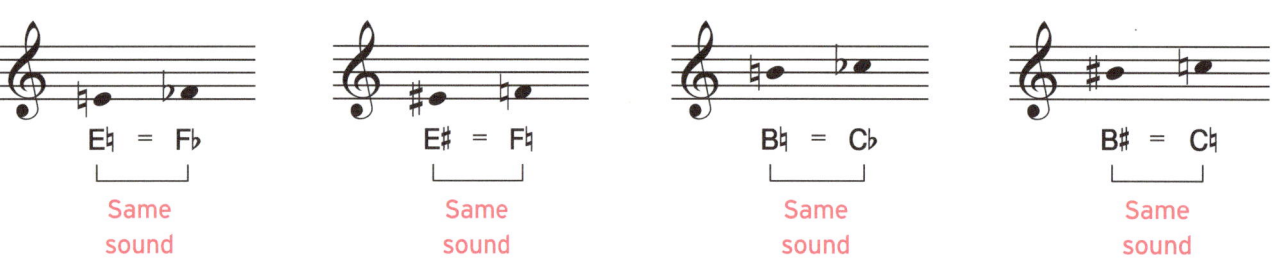

 **Summary**

Initially, it can seem confusing that there are different names for the same thing. However, when we look at the major scale, it will become clear when it is appropriate to use a sharp, natural, or flat.

For the moment, the important thing to remember is that any letter of the musical alphabet is natural unless specified otherwise. If the note is raised by a semitone, it becomes sharp and if it is lowered by a semitone it becomes flat.

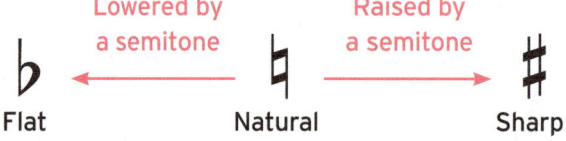

Musical Building Blocks

Exercise: Enharmonic Notes

Write down an enharmonic equivalent for each note below.

Example:

This note is an F♯, written in the treble clef. We know that F♯ is a semitone higher than F natural.

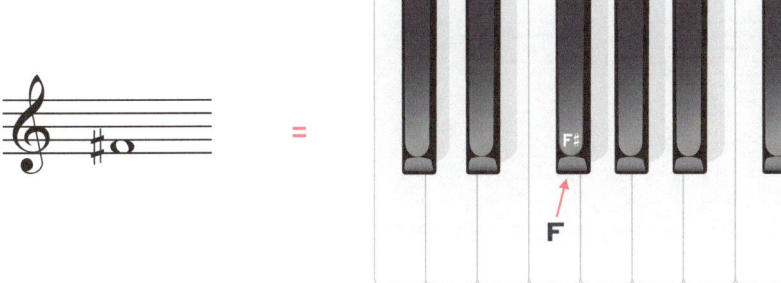

Another name for this note would be G♭, which is a semitone lower than G natural.

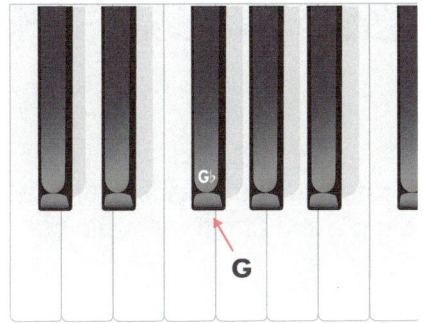

G is the second line up from the bottom on the treble clef and a 'flat' sign needs to be added to the left-hand side of the note.

Exercise 1

Write down an enharmonic equivalent for each note below. Make sure you consider whether the notes are written in the treble or the bass clef. There is a Keyboard Diagram in the Appendix of this book to help you with this exercise.

1    2    3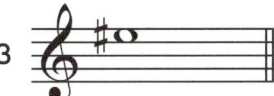

4    5 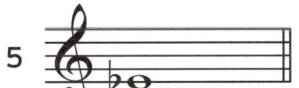   6

Exercise 2

1. Write a chromatic scale from C to C an octave higher, with all the accidentals as **sharps**.

2. Write a chromatic scale from C to C an octave higher, with all the accidentals as **flats**.

Answers can be found online, see page 8 for details.

Tones and Semitones

Semitones

In Western music, a semitone (or half step) is the smallest distance between one note and another. For example, on the piano this would be the very next black or white note, above or below. An example of a semitone would be C to C♯, E to F, or B♭ to B.

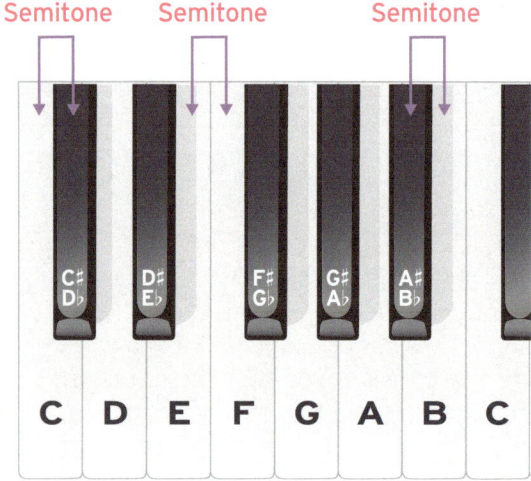

Listen to this track which demonstrates these three sets of semitones (C to C♯, E to F, or B♭ to B) on the piano. Semitones can sound tense and close, almost like they're fighting together. They're often used by composers or songwriters to add tension.

 2.03 Semitones on Piano

Musical Building Blocks

This concept is shown on a piano on page 54, but applies to all instruments.

On the guitar fretboard, semitones are found by playing the very next fret in either direction. For example, an E can be found on the 4th string on the second fret. To move one semitone up from E, you move further up the neck by one fret to F. To move down one semitone from E, you move down the neck by one fret to D♯. The same principle applies to the bass guitar.

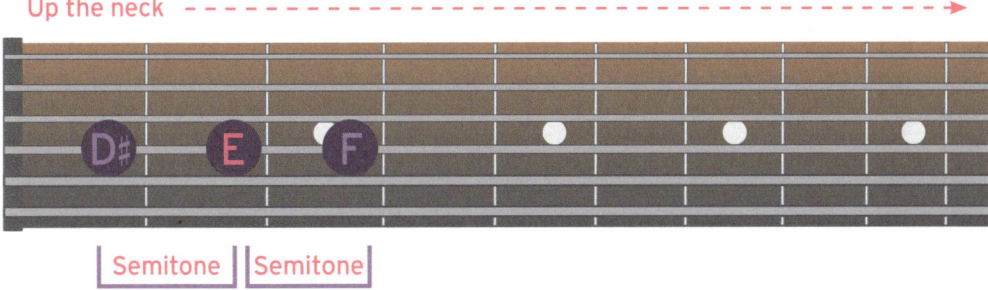

Listen to this track which demonstrates moving up and down a semitone from an E on an electric guitar, followed by a bass guitar (E - F - E - D♯ - E).

 2.04 Semitones on Guitar & Bass Guitar

 **Spotlight**

Tones and semitones are often referred to as 'intervals' – the distance between one note and another.

Tones

A tone (or whole step) is the distance of two semitones. Below are some examples of tones found on the piano (C to D, E to F#, and A♭ to B♭, or G# to A#).

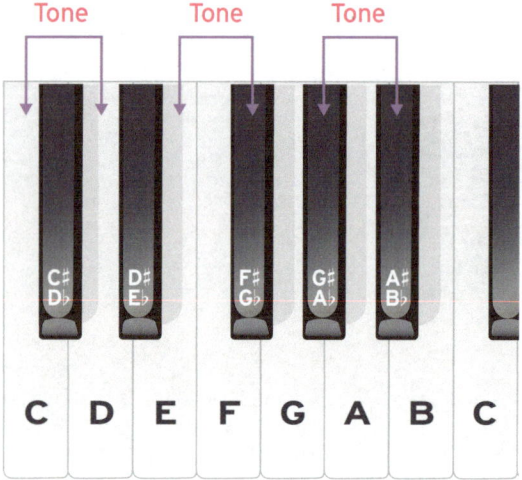

Listen to this track which demonstrates these tones played on a piano (C to D, E to F#, and A♭ to B♭).

 2.05 Tones on Piano

On a guitar fretboard, tones can be found by moving two frets in either direction. For example, a C can be found on the 5th string on the 3rd fret. To move one tone up from C, you move further up the neck by two frets to D. To move down one tone from C, you move down the neck by two frets to B♭. The same principle applies to the bass guitar.

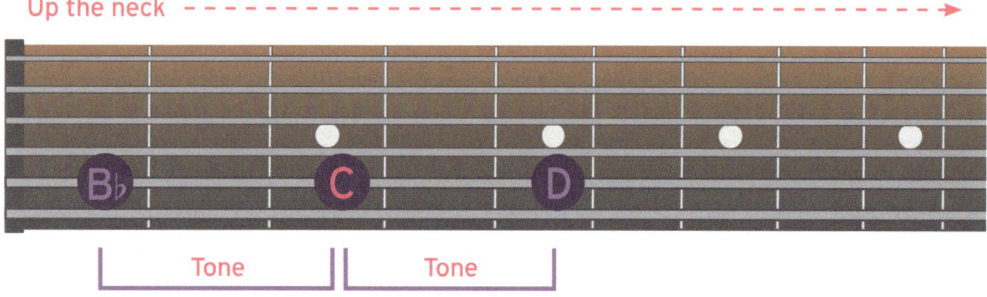

Listen to this track which demonstrates moving up and down a tone from a C, on an electric guitar, followed by a bass guitar (C - D - C - B♭ - C).

 2.06 Tones on Guitar & Bass Guitar

 **Extra Info**

Don't forget to try singing along with the audio tracks – this will really help you to recognise the difference between a tone and a semitone aurally, which will be a very useful skill as we begin to look at more complex intervals and chords.

Musical Building Blocks

 **Questions**

Here are some questions on the topics covered so far.

There is a Keyboard Diagram in the Appendix of this book to help you with this exercise.

1. What is the name for the **smallest interval** between one note and another? ....

2. What note is a **semitone higher** than F#? ....

3. What note is a **semitone lower** than B♭? ....

4. E♭ is a **semitone higher** than which note? ....

5. A **tone** is made up of how many semitones? ....

6. What note is a **tone higher** than G? ....

7. D♭ is a **tone lower** than which note? ....

8. What note is a **tone higher** than A? ....

9. Which two pairs of notes have **no semitones** between them? ....

10. How many frets do you need to move up the neck of a guitar to play a **semitone higher**? ....

Answers can be found online, see page 8 for details.

Scales

Scales are the building blocks of music and can help us create melodies and chords as they show us which notes fit well together.

A scale is a set of notes which in this book will usually be arranged in ascending order. Musicians tend to practise scales by ascending and then descending the order of notes. There are two main types of scale: major and minor. Let's look at major scales first.

The Major Scale Formula

Major scales have seven different notes and, using a combination of tones (T) and semitones (S), there is a simple pattern to work out any major scale, starting on any note.

T - T - S - T - T - T - S

Here is a major scale starting on C (C major), which uses this pattern. Listen to this track which demonstrates the C major scale ascending and descending on the piano, followed by the guitar and bass.

 2.07 C Major Scale on Piano, Guitar & Bass Guitar

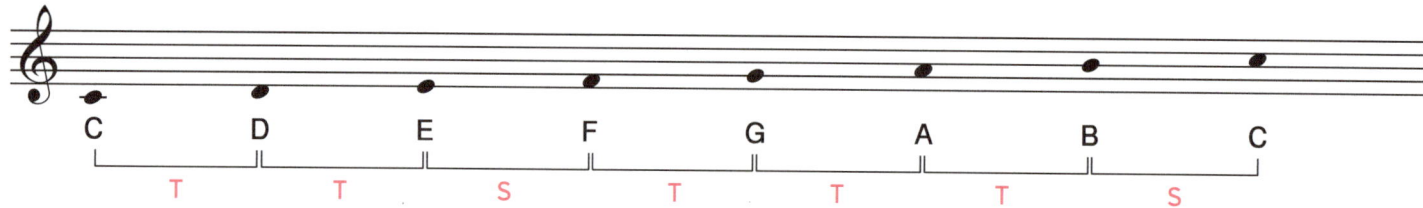

In C major the semitones fall between E and F, and B and C. The C major scale is unique in that it falls on all the white notes on the piano and is the only major scale that doesn't include any sharps or flats.

The first note of a major scale is sometimes referred to as the keynote. Notice how in a major scale there are two keynotes, one at the bottom of the scale (the starting note) and one at the top of the scale (the final note). These notes are an octave apart.

 **Extra Info**

Remember that a semitone (or half step) is the distance between one note and the very next note on either side. A tone (or whole step) is the distance of two semitones.

Musical Building Blocks

Let's build another major scale, using the same pattern of tones and semitones. Let's start this scale on D.

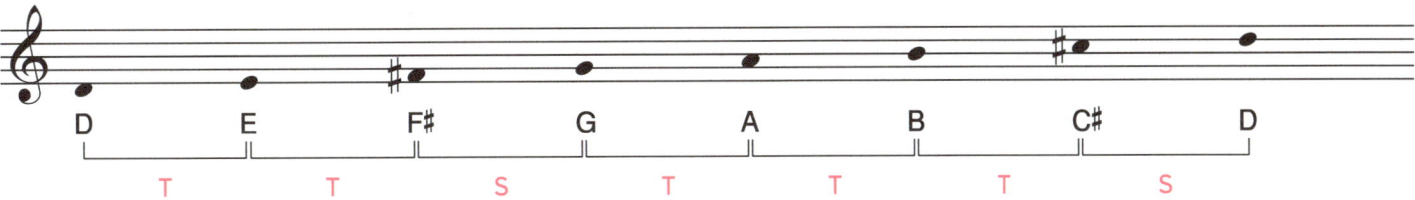

D major has two sharps: F♯ (which is a tone above E) and C♯ (a tone above B).

Spotlight

So why is it F♯ rather than G♭? Also, why is it C♯ rather than D♭?

This is because every letter of the musical alphabet (A, B, C, D, E, F, G) needs to be included within a major scale. If we referred to the F♯ as a G♭, there would be no note with the letter F.

If we referred to the C♯ as D♭, there would be no note with the letter C.

This is an important rule to remember: every letter of the musical alphabet must be included within each scale.

Let's build another major scale: B♭ major.

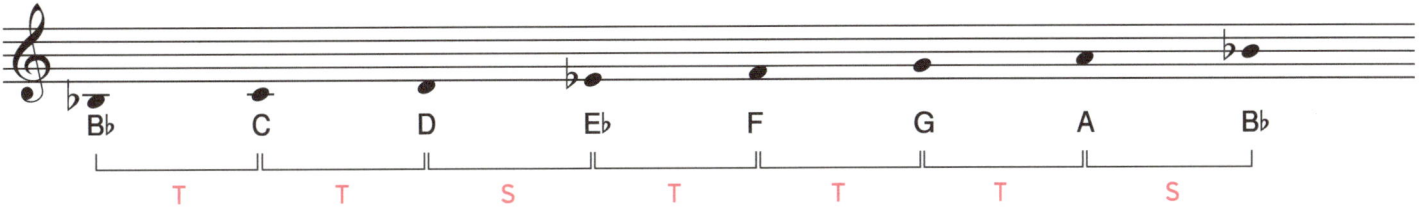

After building this scale, we can see that B♭ major has two flats: B♭ and E♭. We need to include a B♭ as this is the starting note (keynote) of the scale. E♭ has also been included because it is a semitone away from D.

Exercise: Building Major Scales

Build the following major scales using the formula: T - T - S - T - T - T - S.

The first note for each has been provided for you.

Exercise 1: G major

Exercise 2: A major

Exercise 3: E♭ major

Exercise 4: A♭ major. Slightly trickier! Look at the clef…

Exercise 5: E major. Slightly trickier! Look at the clef…

Answers can be found online, see page 8 for details.

Musical Building Blocks

Degrees of the Scale

Each note of a scale is often referred to as a 'degree'. Each degree has a different feeling, weight, and relation to the other notes in the scale. It can also lay the foundations for recognising and creating chord sequences, bass lines, and other musical ideas.

Each degree can be numbered, for example, the first note would be the 1st degree, the second note would be the 2nd degree, and so on. The 8th degree of the scale (in this case, C) is the same as the 1st but an octave higher, so we go back to calling this the 1st degree of the scale, and so on.

Here is an F major scale, built using the same formula.

As well as numbering the scale degrees, there are other ways of describing the various steps in a scale. The 1st degree of the scale is also referred to as the tonic. Five notes above the tonic is the dominant and five notes below the tonic is the subdominant ('sub' meaning 'under' in Latin). When counting the distances between notes, you include the note you start on; for example, the distance between F and C is five notes – F, G, A, B♭, C.
While the terms below are more 'traditional', they are still frequently used by many musicians.

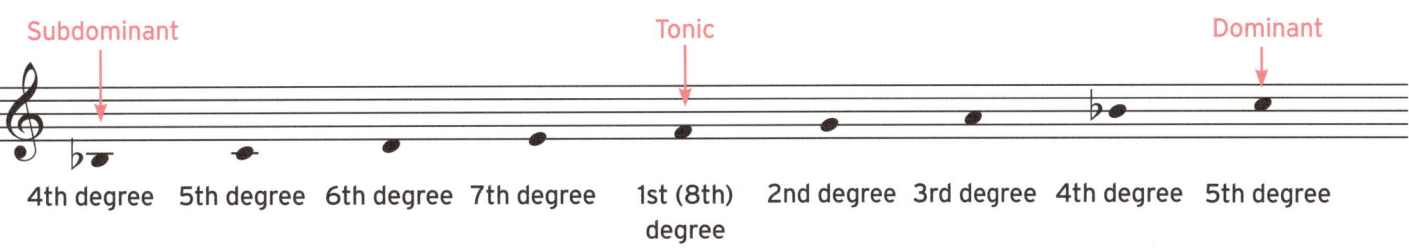

 **Spotlight**

Notice that the scale above has been written differently from the other examples. While this is still the scale of F major, F has been written in the middle of the scale, to show the notes above and below the tonic. The dominant is a 5th above the tonic, and the subdominant is a 5th below the tonic.

The mediant is a 3rd above the tonic, and the submediant is a 3rd below the tonic.

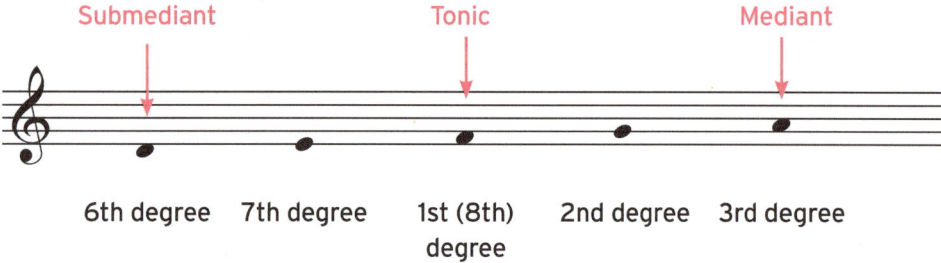

The supertonic is the note above the tonic ('super' meaning 'above' in Latin). The leading note is the note below the tonic because it leads us back to the 1st degree of the scale. This note has a strong pull towards the first note of the scale, creating a sense of resolution and giving it its distinctive name.

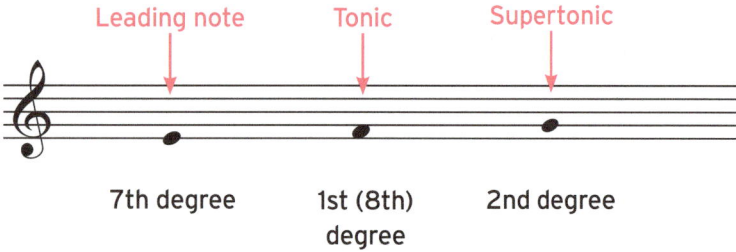

So far, all these terms have been described with the tonic in the middle of the scale. Here they are in sequence, if we arrange the scale in ascending order, with the tonic as the first note.

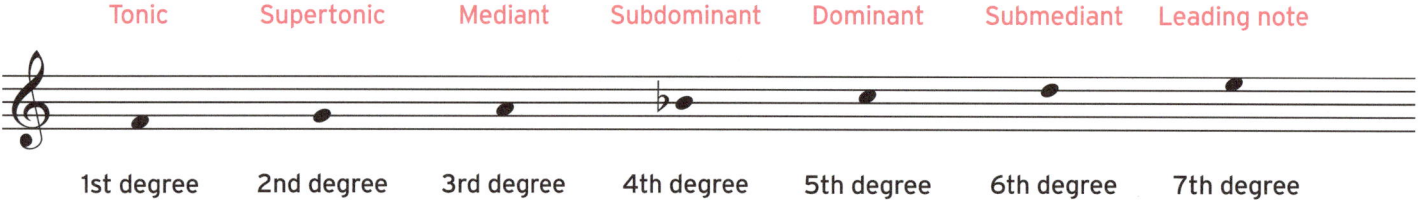

While all these terms are important to understand, the three you'll encounter the most are the tonic, subdominant, and dominant. We'll look at these in more detail later in this book.

Spotlight

These names (tonic, dominant, subdominant etc.) are often used in a more traditional/classical setting, however its useful to understand the various ways that musicians refer to the steps in a scale.

Understanding terms like 'tonic' and 'dominant' instead of just numbering scale degrees makes it easier for musicians to communicate and convey musical ideas. These terms provide a quick and clear way to describe the importance and function of specific notes in a scale, which helps in composing, improvising, and collaborating.

Musical Building Blocks

 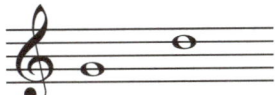

Exercise: Degrees of the Scale

In each question, two notes are given. Using the scale degrees (subdominant, dominant etc.) **identify the relationship between the higher note and the lower note.**

Make sure you check the clef before you begin.

Example:

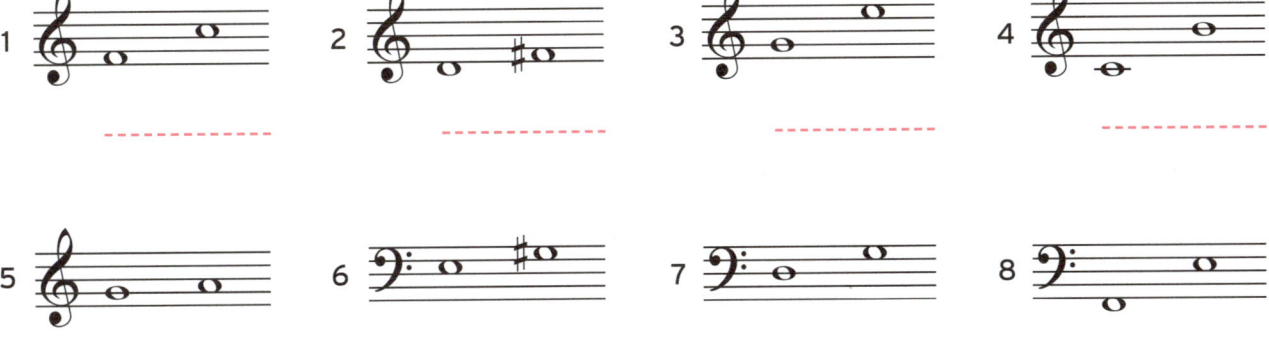

The bottom note is a G and the top note is a D. D is the 5th degree of the G major scale and is therefore the dominant.

Answers can be found online, see page 8 for details.

Intervals

An interval is the distance between two notes. Intervals are useful as they can help you label and analyse the differences between two pitches within a scale, melody, or chord.

Intervals can either be referred to as **harmonic** or **melodic**. In other words, if the two notes are played together, this creates harmony and is therefore a harmonic interval. If the two notes are played one after the other, this creates a melody and is a melodic interval.

When describing an interval, there are two important pieces of information – the type of interval and the size of the interval. For example, the interval between C and E is a major 3rd; 'major' tells us the type of interval, and the '3rd' tells us the size of the interval.

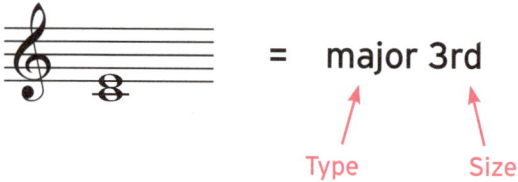

Interval Size

Let's begin by looking at the size of the interval, which is usually an ordinal number (2nd, 3rd, 4th, 5th etc.) The simplest way to calculate the size is to use the musical alphabet and count the distance between the lower note and the upper note, however, you must include the lower note when counting.

For example, the interval between A and D is a 4th because there are four letters of the musical alphabet between A and D (A, B, C, and D).

Let's look at another example, this time using the stave. Another way to calculate the size of an interval is to count the lines and spaces between two notes. For example, the interval of C to G is a 5th because there are five lines and spaces between C and G (C, D, E, F, and G).

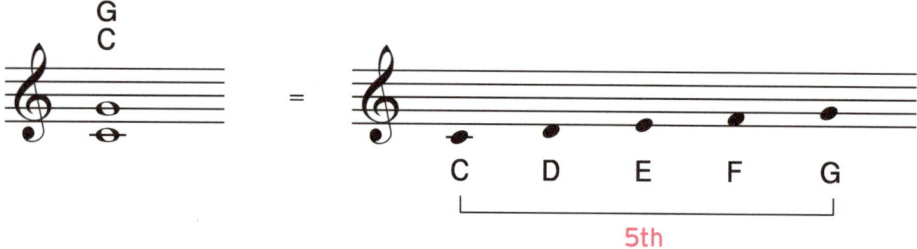

Musical Building Blocks

All the possible interval sizes within an octave are shown below. Notice that if the two notes are the same, they are either labelled as unison (unis.), rather than a 1st, and an octave (8ve), rather than an 8th.

Listen to this track which demonstrates all of these intervals played harmonically (notes played together) and then melodically (one note after the other).

 2.08 Intervals from C Played Harmonically and Melodically

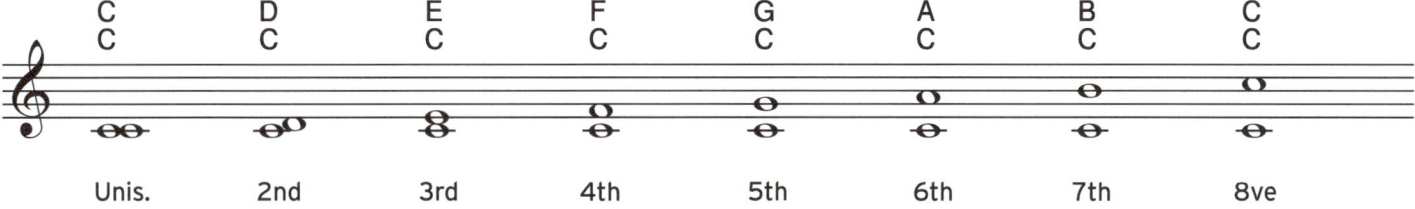

It doesn't matter what the lower note is, even if there are accidentals (♭ or ♯) next to some of the notes, the process is still the same – you can use the musical alphabet, or the number of lines and spaces on the stave, to work out the size of the interval.

For example, here are the same intervals with E♭ as the lower note. Listen to this track which demonstrates all of these intervals played harmonically and then melodically.

 2.09 Intervals from E♭ Played Harmonically and Melodically

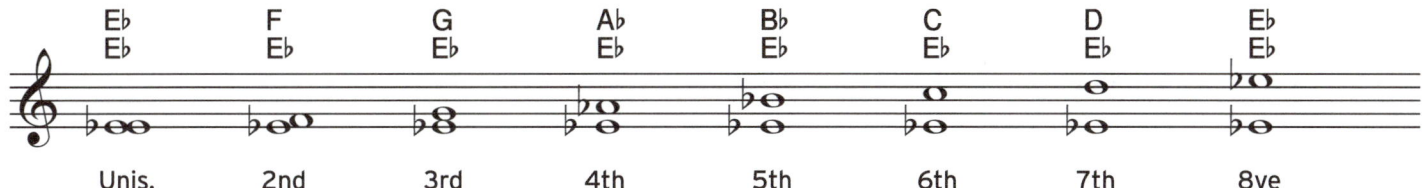

 **Extra Info**

Consonant intervals within the major scale are those that sound pleasant and stable. These intervals create a sense of harmony and are often used to create pleasing melodies and chords. In the major scale, the most consonant intervals are the unison, 4th, 5th, 6th and octave. They have a sense of resolution and feel comfortable to the ear.

Dissonant intervals within the major scale are those that sound tense and unstable. These intervals create a feeling of tension and sometimes seek resolution to a more consonant interval. In the major scale, the most dissonant intervals are the 7th and the 2nd and these intervals can create a sense of unease.

It's important to remember that whether an interval is considered consonant or dissonant can be subjective, as individual preferences and cultural contexts play a role in how we perceive these musical combinations.

Exercise: What's the Size of the Interval?

Part 1

Calculate the size of the following intervals. For the moment, ignore any sharps or flats and use the musical alphabet, or the number of lines and spaces, to calculate the size of the interval.

Remember to always include and count from the lower note when working out the size of the interval.

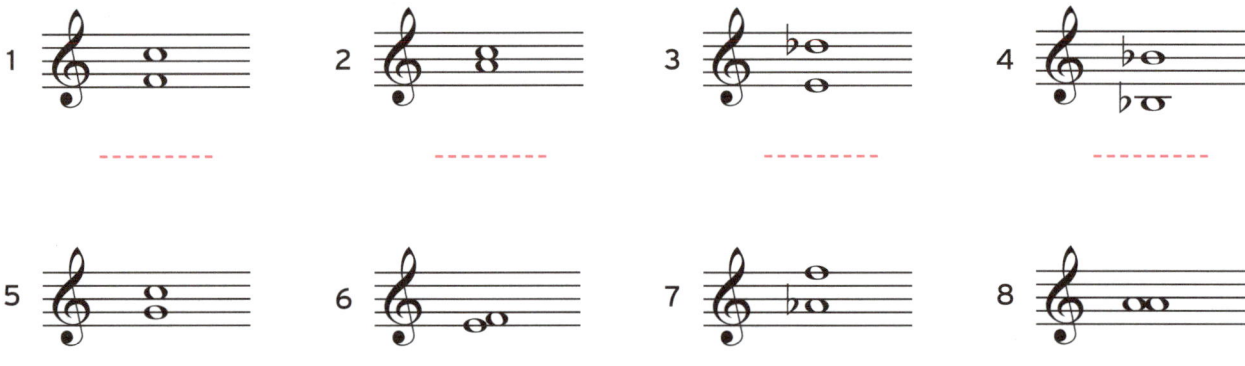

Part 2

Calculate the size of the following intervals by listening to the tracks.

Sing a scale from the lower note to the higher note whilst counting the degrees of the scale, eg, 1, 2, 3, 4 = 4th. The lower note will be played followed by the higher note. The intervals will either be a unison, 4th, 5th or octave.

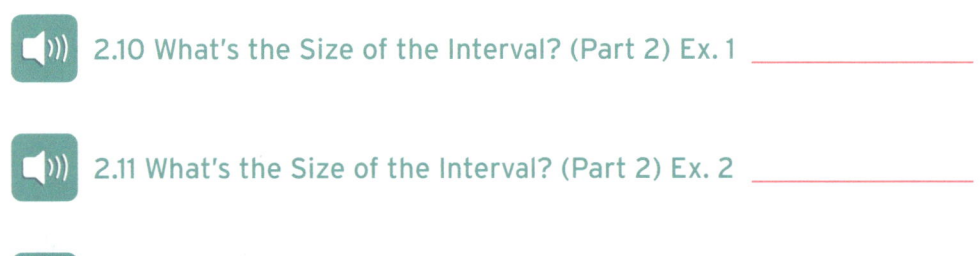

2.10 What's the Size of the Interval? (Part 2) Ex. 1 _____

2.11 What's the Size of the Interval? (Part 2) Ex. 2 _____

2.12 What's the Size of the Interval? (Part 2) Ex. 3 _____

2.13 What's the Size of the Interval? (Part 2) Ex. 4 _____

2.14 What's the Size of the Interval? (Part 2) Ex. 5 _____

Musical Building Blocks

Part 3

Calculate the size of the following intervals by listening to the tracks.

Sing a scale from the lower note to the higher note whilst counting the degrees of the scale.
The lower note will be played followed by the higher note. The intervals will either be a 2nd, 3rd, 6th, or 7th.

 2.15 What's the Size of the Interval? (Part 3) Ex. 1 _____

 2.16 What's the Size of the Interval? (Part 3) Ex. 2 _____

 2.17 What's the Size of the Interval? (Part 3) Ex. 3 _____

 2.18 What's the Size of the Interval? (Part 3) Ex. 4 _____

 2.19 What's the Size of the Interval? (Part 3) Ex. 5 _____

Answers can be found online, see page 8 for details.

 ## Exercise: Major or Minor Intervals

Write the interval of a 3rd above each of these notes of the C major scale and state whether they are major or minor.

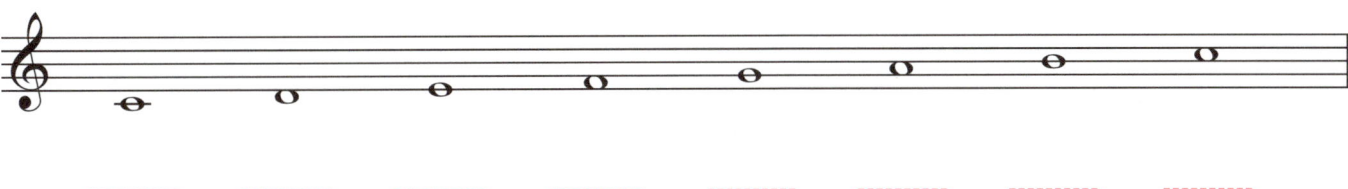

Answers can be found online, see page 8 for details.

Interval Type

To work out the **type** of interval we need to use the major scale starting from the lower note.

If the lower note of an interval is a C, and the upper note exists within the C major scale, then this will either be a perfect or a major interval.

- Unison, 4th, 5th, and octave intervals are perfect.
- 2nd, 3rd, 6th, and 7th intervals are described as major.

Listen to this track which demonstrates all these intervals played harmonically and then melodically.

 2.20 Intervals from C Played Harmonically and Melodically

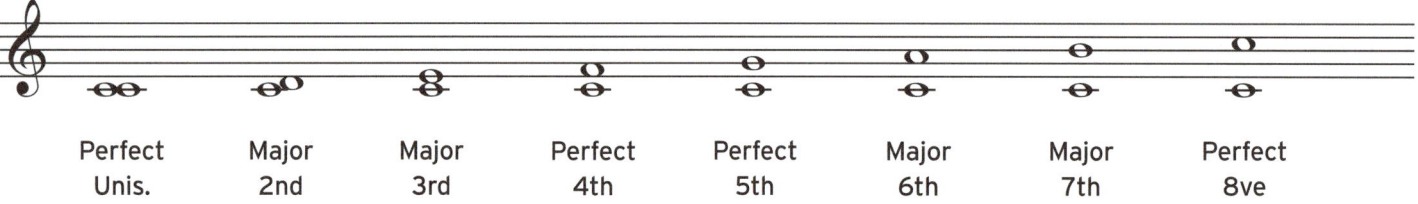

| Perfect | Major | Major | Perfect | Perfect | Major | Major | Perfect |
| Unis. | 2nd | 3rd | 4th | 5th | 6th | 7th | 8ve |

Let's do the same thing with E as our lower note. As all the upper notes in the example below exist within the E major scale, we know that the intervals are either going to be perfect or major.

Listen to this track which demonstrates all of these intervals played harmonically and then melodically.

 2.21 Intervals from E Played Harmonically and Melodically

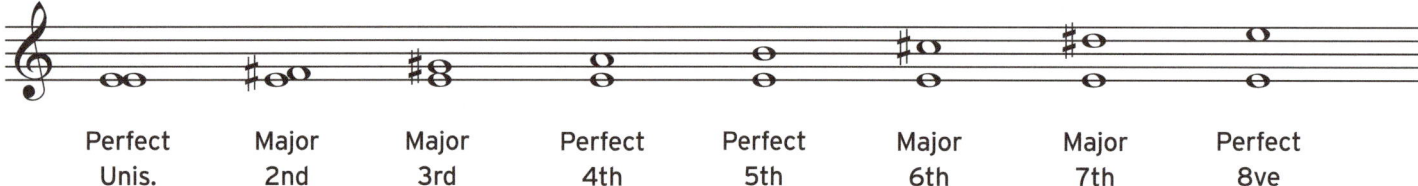

| Perfect | Major | Major | Perfect | Perfect | Major | Major | Perfect |
| Unis. | 2nd | 3rd | 4th | 5th | 6th | 7th | 8ve |

Musical Building Blocks

 **Exercise: Perfect or Major?**

Work out the following intervals. You will need to calculate the size of the interval and the type of interval (perfect or major). Remember to check the clef before you begin – not all the questions are written using the treble clef.

Example:

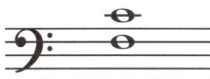

The two notes here are F and C (notice that this example is written in bass clef). There are **five** letters of the musical alphabet between F and C (F, G, A, B, and C), so the size of the interval is a **5th**.

Now we need to work out the type of interval. Using the T-T-S-T-T-T-S formula, we can construct our F major scale:

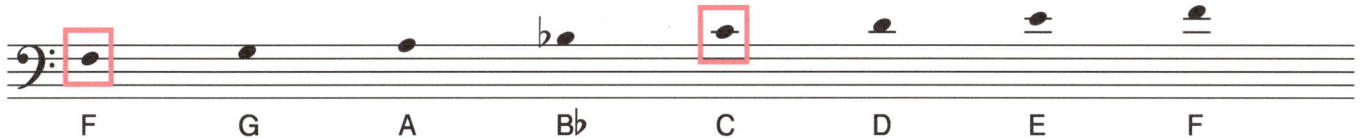

We know that 5ths within the major scale are called 'perfect' – C is the 5th note of the F major scale. Therefore, this interval is a **perfect 5th**.

To help you connect the sounds of these intervals with the notation, listen to this track which demonstrates these intervals played on a piano. Each interval is played twice.

 2.22 Intervals (Perfect or Major?)

Exercises:

Answers can be found online, see page 8 for details.

Lowering/Raising a Major Interval

Let's look at what happens when the upper note in a major interval is lowered or raised by a semitone.

If the upper note is lowered, the interval becomes *minor*. So, for example, C to E is a major 3rd, so a minor 3rd is C to E♭ (the 3rd has been lowered by a semitone). Only major intervals can become minor (2nds, 3rds, 6ths, and 7ths).

Listen to this track which demonstrates a major 3rd followed by a minor 3rd.

 2.23 Major 3rd Followed by a Minor 3rd

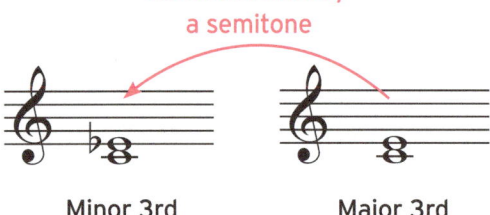

Spotlight

Remember that both intervals are types of 3rd because the main letter of the musical alphabet has remained the same – E and E♭ (both are Es).

If the upper note of a major interval is raised by a semitone, then the interval becomes *augmented*. For example, C to E is a major 3rd, so an augmented 3rd is C to E♯ (the 3rd has been raised by a semitone).

Listen to this track which demonstrates a major 3rd, followed by an augmented 3rd.

 2.24 Major 3rd Followed by an Augmented 3rd

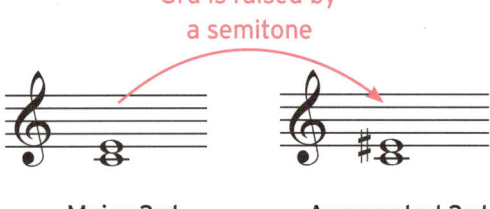

Spotlight

Again, both intervals are types of 3rds because the main letter of the musical alphabet has remained the same – E and E♯ (both are Es).

E♯ isn't a particularly common note – however, it's important to understand the concept of how intervals are named.

Musical Building Blocks

The diagram below highlights how all the major intervals within an octave (2nd, 3rd, 6th, and 7th) can become minor or augmented by lowering or raising the upper note by a semitone.

Use the audio tracks below to help you begin to recognise these intervals by ear. Each interval (2nd, 3rd, 6th, and 7th) is played minor, then major, followed by augmented.

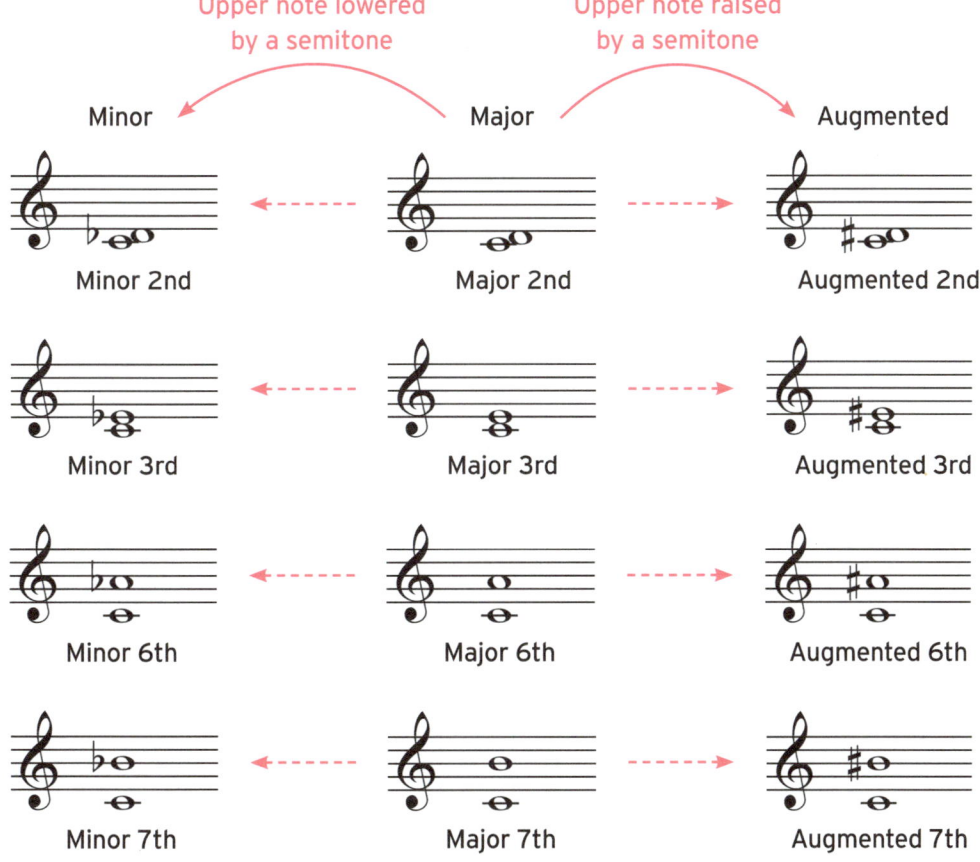

Listen to these tracks, which align the to notation above:

 2.25 Minor, Major, and Augmented 2nds   2.26 Minor, Major, and Augmented 3rds

 2.27 Minor, Major, and Augmented 6ths   2.28 Minor, Major, and Augmented 7ths

Extra Info

Some of the intervals here are rare – for example, it's unlikely that you'll encounter many augmented 3rds or 7ths. These intervals could be respelled using enharmonic equivalents (an augmented 3rd, is likely to be written as a perfect 4th, and an augmented 7th is likely to be written as an octave).

However, it's important to understand the principles behind how intervals work.

Spotlight

Sometimes musicians describe an augmented interval as 'raised', for example, a 'raised 6th', rather than an 'augmented 6th'.

Minor intervals can also be referred to as 'flat', for example, a 'flat 3rd', or a 'flat 7th'. This is something to be aware of; however, to be completely accurate with terminology, augmented and minor are the appropriate terms.

Exercise: Minor, Major, or Augmented?

Work out the following intervals.

Remember to check the clef before you begin – not all the questions are written using the treble clef.

Example:

The two notes here are F and D♭. There are **six** letters of the musical alphabet between F and D♭ (F, G, A, B, C and D), so the size of the interval is a **6th**.

Now we need to work out the type of interval. Using the T-T-S-T-T-T-S formula, we need to construct our F major scale. You can use the scales in the Appendix to help you.

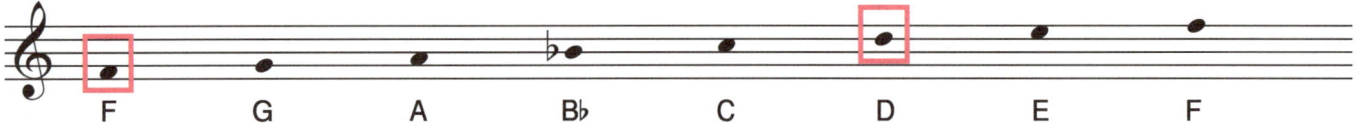

D natural is the sixth note of the F major scale. If a major interval is flattened, then it becomes minor. Therefore, this interval is a **minor 6th**.

Exercises on next page.

Musical Building Blocks

 2.29 Intervals (Minor, Major or Augmented?)

To help you connect the sounds of these intervals with the notation, listen to this track which demonstrates these intervals played on a piano. Each interval is played twice.

Work out the following intervals.

All the intervals are either 2nds, 3rds, 6ths, or 7ths. You will need to work out whether the intervals are minor, major, or augmented.

Exercises:

1  2  3  4

5  6  7  8

Answers can be found online, see page 8 for details.

Lowering/Raising a Perfect Interval

So, what happens to a perfect interval (unis., 4th, 5th, and octave) if the upper note is raised or lowered by a semitone?

If the upper note in a perfect interval is lowered by a semitone, then it becomes diminished. For example, C to G is a perfect 5th, so a diminished 5th is C to G♭ (the 5th has been lowered by a semitone).

Listen to this track which demonstrates a perfect 5th, followed by a diminished 5th.

 2.30 Perfect 5th Followed by a Diminished 5th

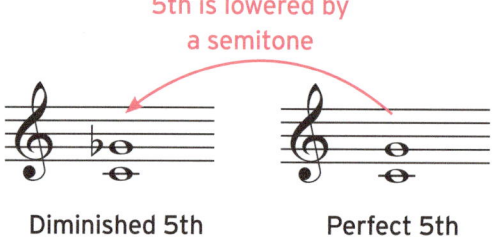

If the upper note in a 'perfect' interval is raised by a semitone, then it becomes augmented. For example, we know C to G is a perfect 5th, so an augmented 5th is C to G♯ (the 5th has been raised by a semitone).

Listen to this track which demonstrates a perfect 5th, followed by an augmented 5th.

 2.31 Perfect 5th Followed by an Augmented 5th

Exercise: Augmented, Diminished or Perfect

Add accidentals to make these 5ths into either augmented, diminished or perfect 5ths.

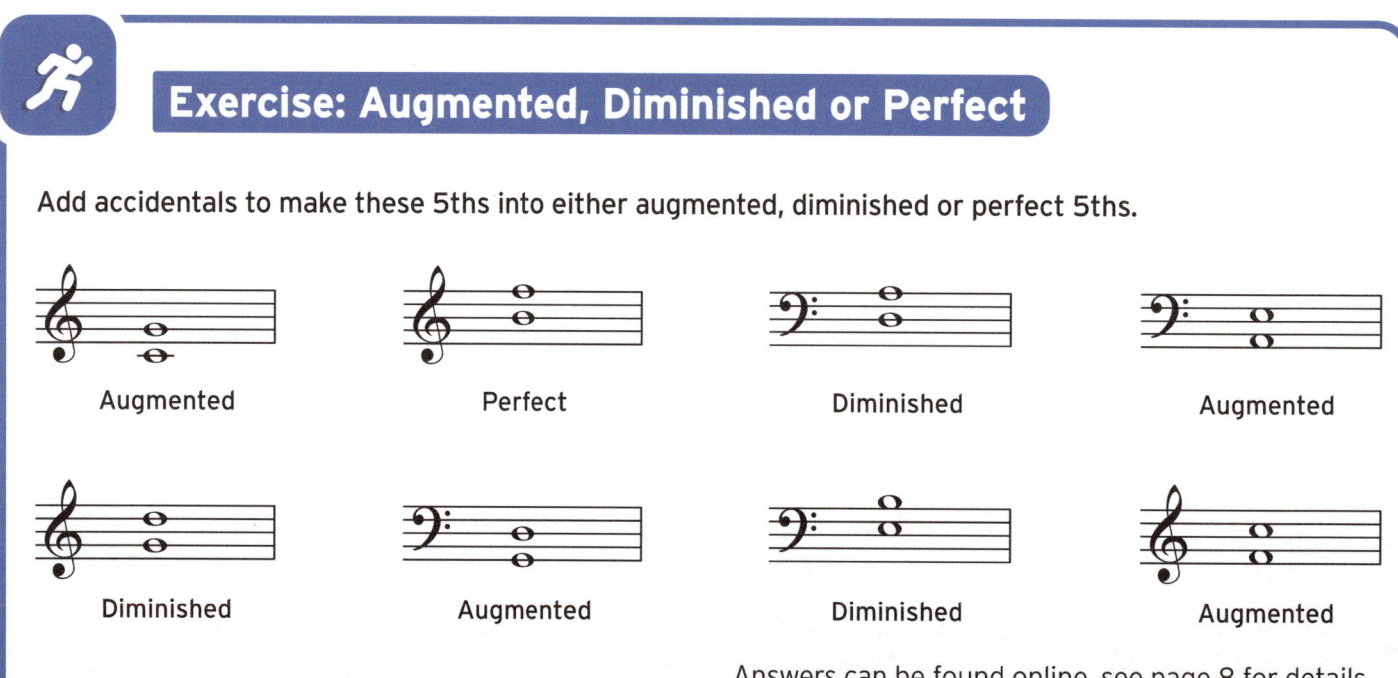

Answers can be found online, see page 8 for details.

Musical Building Blocks

The diagram below highlights how all the perfect intervals within an octave (unis., 4th, 5th, and 8ve) can become diminished or augmented by lowering or raising the upper note by a semitone.

Use the audio tracks below to help you begin to recognise these intervals by ear. Each interval is played diminished, then perfect, followed by augmented.

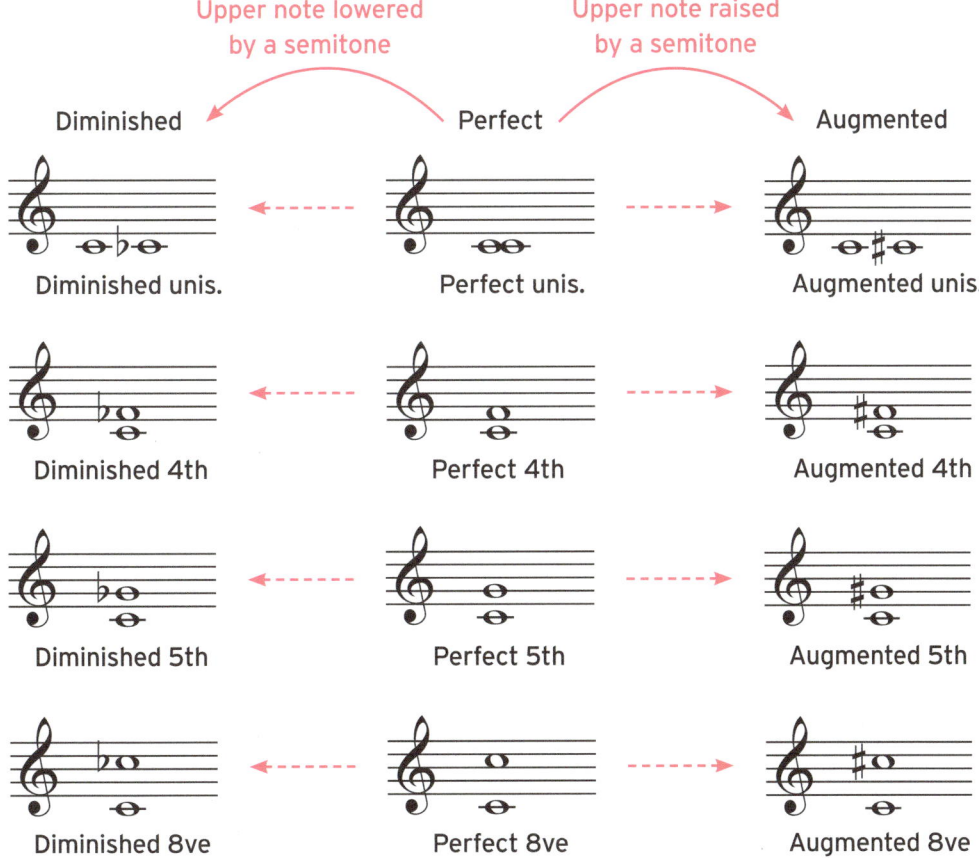

Listen to these tracks, which align the to notation above:

 2.32 Diminished, Perfect, and Augmented Unisons

 2.33 Diminished, Perfect, and Augmented 4ths

 2.34 Diminished, Perfect, and Augmented 5ths

 2.35 Diminished, Perfect, and Augmented 8ves

 **Extra Info**

Again, there are some very rare intervals here. It's very unlikely you'll ever encounter a diminished unison, diminished 4th, or diminished octave – these intervals could be respelled using enharmonic equivalents. However, it's important to understand the principles behind how they work.

The augmented 4th is usually referred to as a tritone – this is because it is made up of three tones ('tri' meaning three). For example, D – G♯ is an interval of a tritone. Musicians often call these intervals tritones, rather than augmented 4ths.

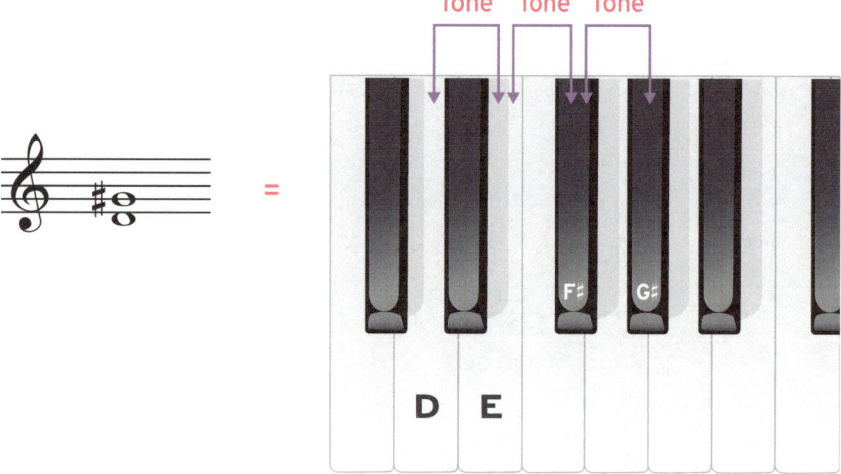

The tritone sits right between a perfect 4th and a perfect 5th – two very consonant intervals. The tritone has a somewhat tense sound. In the past, people thought that the tritone sounded so strange that they called it the 'Devil's Interval' and even believed it brought bad luck. Over time, composers and songwriters used this interval to add tension in the music.

Exercise: Tritones

Add a tritone above each of these notes. Depending on the given note, you may find it easier to add a diminished 5th rather than an augmented 4th.

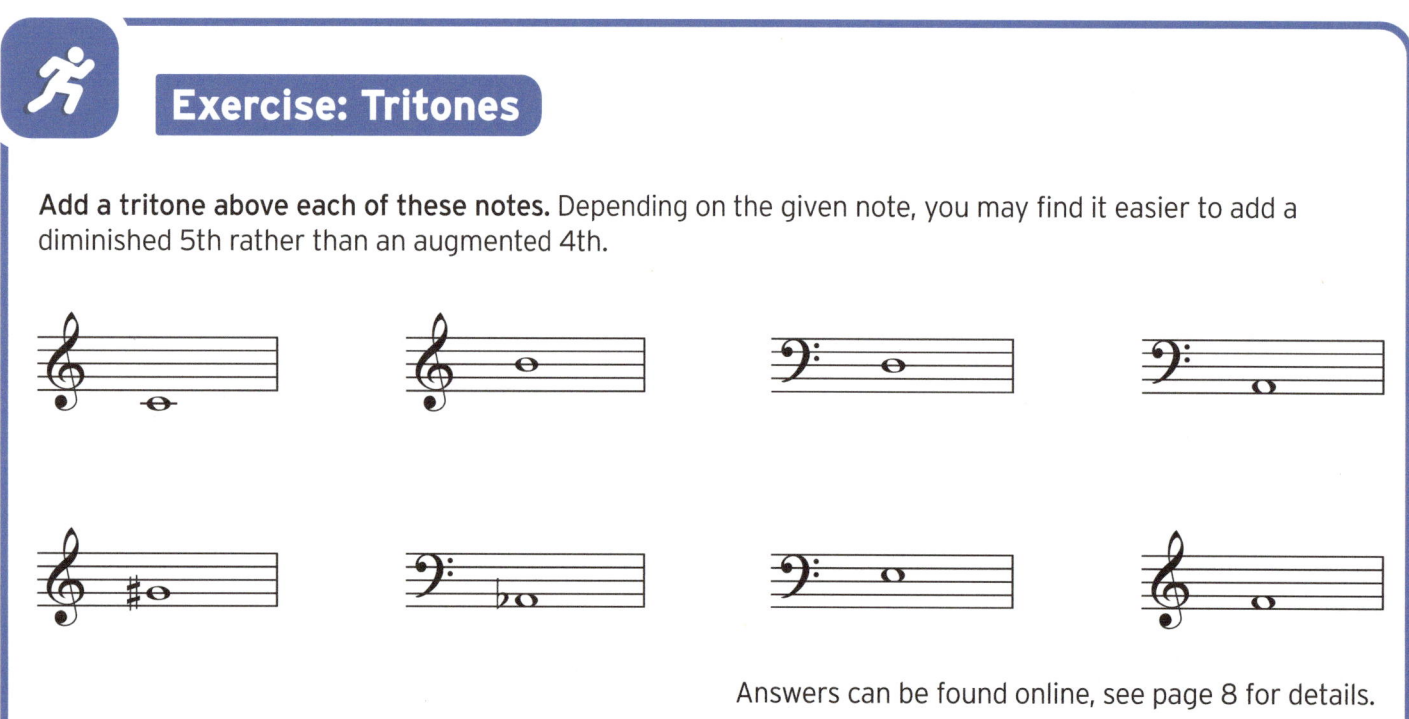

Answers can be found online, see page 8 for details.

Musical Building Blocks

Exercise: Diminished, Perfect, or Augmented?

Exercise 1

Work out the following intervals. All the intervals are either unisons, 4ths, 5ths, or octaves. You will need to work out whether the intervals are diminished, perfect, or augmented.

Remember to check the clef before you begin – not all the questions are written using the treble clef.

Example:

The two notes here are G and D♭. There are **five** letters of the musical alphabet between G and D♭ (G, A, B, C and D), so the size of the interval is a **5th**.

Now we need to work out the type of interval. Using the T-T-S-T-T-T-S formula, we need to construct our G major scale. You can use the scales in the Appendix to help you.

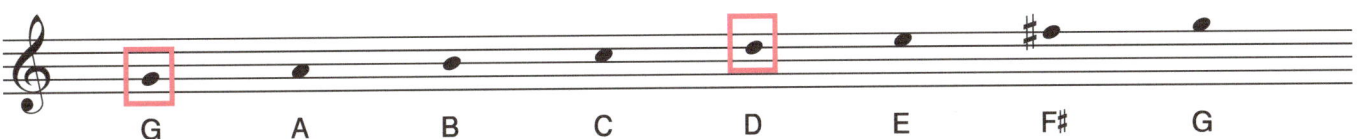

D natural is the 5th note of the G major scale. If a perfect interval is flattened, it becomes diminished. Therefore, this interval is a **diminished 5th**.

 2.36 Intervals (Diminished, Perfect or Augmented?)

Work out the following intervals. All the intervals are either unisons, 4ths, 5ths, or octaves. You will need to work out whether the intervals are diminished, perfect, or augmented.

To help you connect the sounds of these intervals with the notation, listen to this track which demonstrates these intervals played on a piano. Each interval is played twice.

Exercises:

Answers can be found online, see page 8 for details.

Write the following intervals, the lower note is provided for you.

Remember to check the clef before you begin – not all the questions are written using the treble clef.

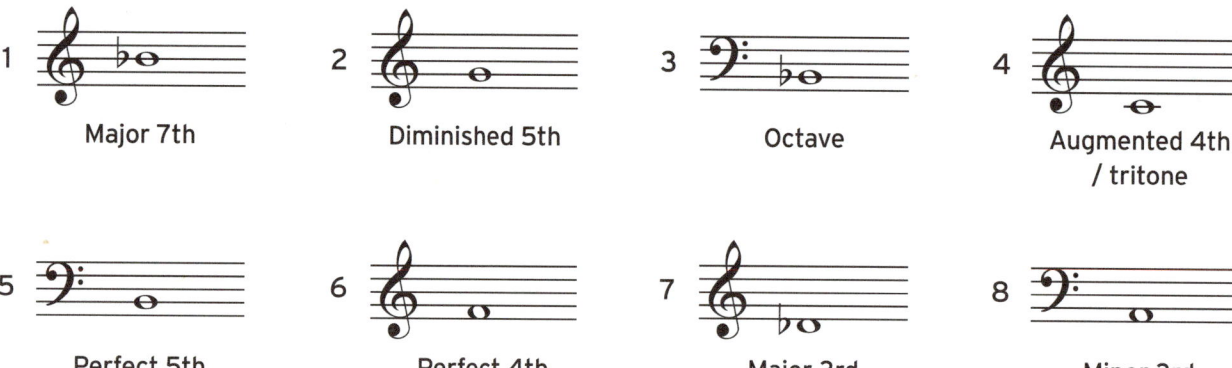

Answers can be found online, see page 8 for details.

 **Extra Info**

Practise singing and playing these intervals to begin to get an idea of what they sound like.

It's important to be able to recognise intervals aurally – for example, it's useful to be able to hear two notes played either harmonically or melodically and then be able to identify the interval.

There are some excellent online resources that can help you practise these skills. If you search for 'free music theory online ear training' there will be several to choose from.

Musical Building Blocks

Summary

Intervals can initially be quite confusing, however, it's important to get to grips with them as they can help with so many aspects of music, including understanding melodies, chords, transposing... the list goes on!

Here are some rules to help you:

- When working out an interval, you always calculate the interval from the lower note to the upper note;
- If the upper note fits within the major scale of the lower note, then the interval is either perfect (unison, 4th, 5th, and octave) or major (2nd, 3rd, 6th, and 7th);
- An interval a semitone smaller than a perfect interval is diminished;
- An interval a semitone smaller than a major interval is minor;
- An interval a semitone larger than a perfect or major interval is augmented.

This diagram highlights how all the intervals within an octave can change by raising or lowering the upper note by a semitone.

The Circle of Fifths

In western music, there are 12 semitones within an octave:

C D♭ D E♭ E F G♭ G A♭ A B♭ B

Shown above is a chromatic scale starting on C, however, a chromatic scale can start on any note. These 12 notes can also be arranged in a circle, known as the circle of fifths.

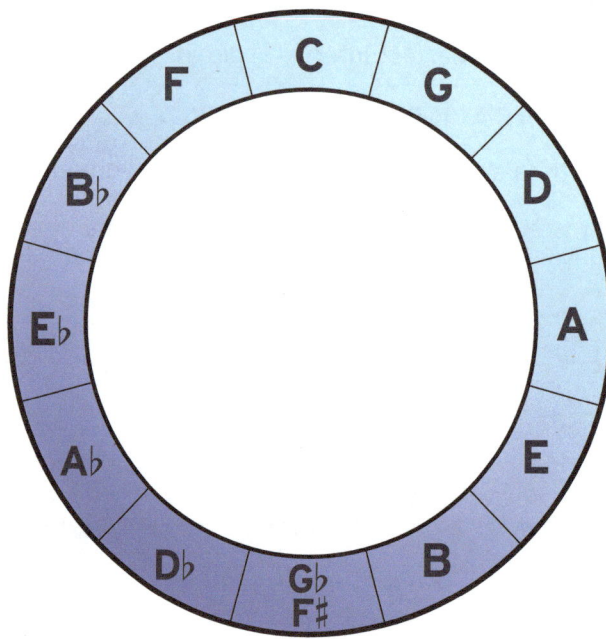

The circle of fifths is a visual tool to help us understand aspects of music theory, including keys, scales, and chords.

So why is it called the circle of fifths? Moving clockwise around the circle, each note is a perfect 5th away from the previous note. Let's look at the first four note names. C sits at the top of the circle and a perfect 5th up from C is G, a perfect 5th up from G is D, a perfect 5th up from D is A, and so on.

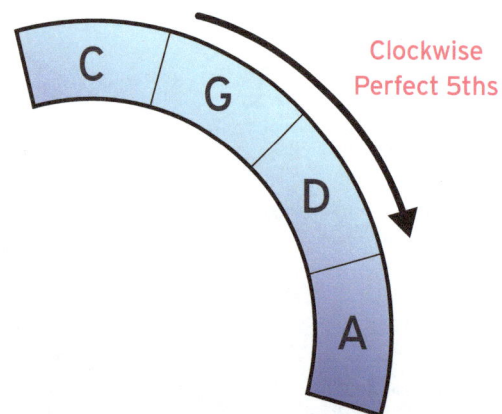

If we carry on adding perfect 5ths to every note moving clockwise, we eventually return to C at the top of the circle.

Musical Building Blocks 81

Listen to this track which demonstrates a chord working its way in a clockwise direction until it returns to C. The sequence is played through twice.

 2.37 Circle of Fifths Progression

 **Extra Info**

You may have also heard this referred to as the 'Cycle of Fifths'.

 **Spotlight**

A quick recap... How do we work out a perfect 5th above a note?

To find a perfect 5th, we can use the major scale formula (T-T-S-T-T-T-S). For example, to find a perfect 5th above D, you need to work out the 5th note of the D major scale. As you only need the 5th note of the scale, you don't need the whole formula, just T-T-S-T. Therefore, a perfect 5th above D is A.

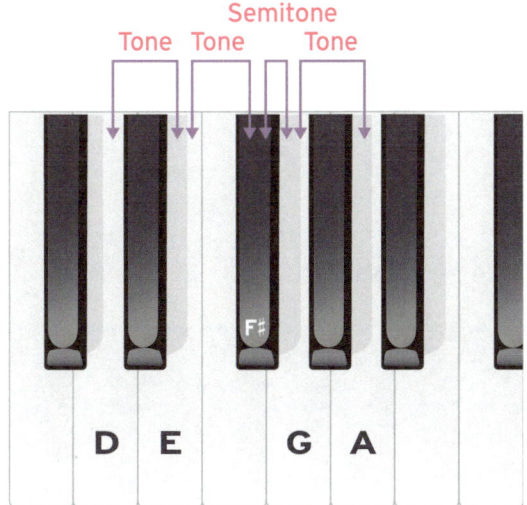

If you play guitar or bass, using one string, you can move two frets up for a tone and one fret up for a semitone.

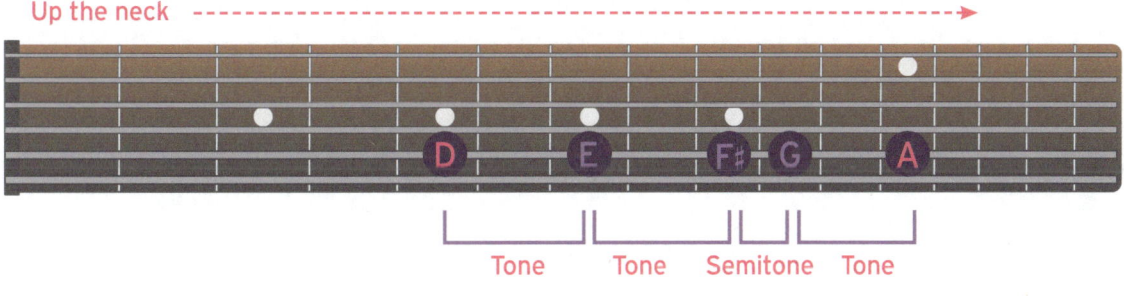

There are many hidden patterns within the circle of fifths. For example, the notes on the left-hand side of the circle (F, B♭, E♭, A♭, D♭) all have flats in their major scales and all the notes on the right-hand side of the circle (G, D, A, E, B) have sharps.

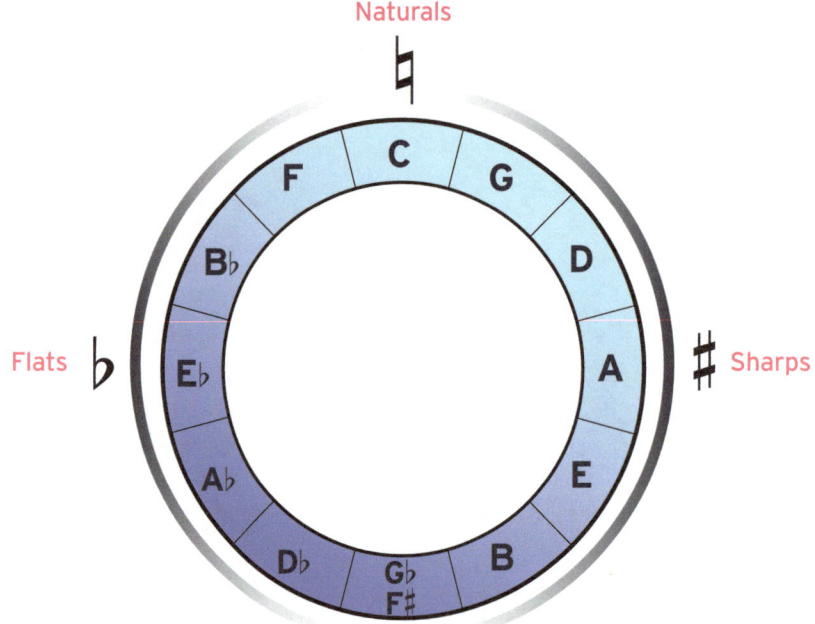

You may be wondering why there are two notes listed at the bottom of the circle (F♯ and G♭).

F♯ and G♭ are enharmonic equivalents with F♯ having sharps in its major scale and G♭ having flats. C is at the top, and is the only major scale that has no sharps or flats, just naturals.

 **Extra Info**

There is a helpful chart in the Appendix with every major scale in treble and bass clef.

Key Signatures

The most common use of the circle of fifths is to recognise and understand keys.

A key is the main group of notes that form the basis of a piece of music. Usually, the notes within a key will make up a scale. For example, if a song was in the key of C major, then most of the notes that make up the melody, bass line, and chords would be from the C major scale.

Each major key has its own key signature, which in notated music appears at the beginning of the stave, after the clef and before the time signature. It also appears on subsequent staves.

Extra Info

The chart in the Appendix with every major scale in the treble and bass clef can help you work out key signatures.

Why Use a Key Signature?

Below is a melody in the key of G major, without a key signature:

The notes in this melody come from the G major scale (G, A, B, C, D, E, F♯, G), and because there is no key signature, every time there is an F♯ in the melody, a sharp sign needs to be written on the left-hand side of the note. The more sharps or flats within a key, the more difficult the music can be to read.

However, if that same melody was written using a G major key signature, it would look like this:

In the above example, a G major key signature is used: a sharp sign is placed on the F line in the treble clef, meaning that all Fs are sharp unless stated otherwise. This is much easier to read!

In the example below, all the Fs would be sharp, even though they are in different octaves.

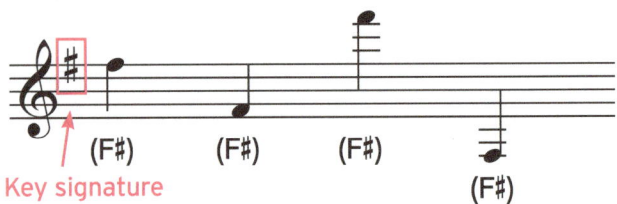

Key signatures make writing music down (notating) much easier. It's important to remember that someone listening to the music wouldn't know whether a key signature had been used – the music would sound the same either way. Key signatures also show the musician what key the song is in.

Extra Info

One of the reasons key signatures were invented was to make writing music by hand more efficient. Using lots of sharp or flat symbols for each note that one needed could be quite costly due to the price of ink. It also made the music look messy.

Key signatures solved this problem by placing just a few sharp or flat symbols at the beginning of each stave, indicating which notes should be played higher or lower throughout. This not only saved ink but also made the music neater.

The Key Signature Clock

A key signature is a bit like a code, it tells you the number of sharps or flats in the key, and from that you can work out the key of the music. Sometimes people just memorise the key signatures, however, it's useful to understand how they are constructed and organised.

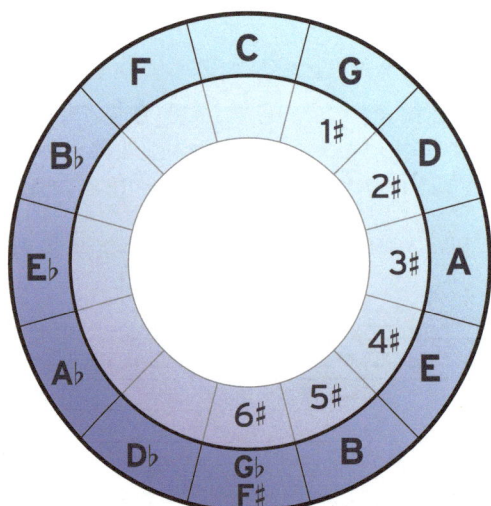

The circle of fifths is often referred to as the 'key signature clock' because the circle is divided into 12 segments. All the keys on the right-hand side of the circle (G, D, A, E, B) have sharps. For example, going clockwise around the circle, G major is at 1 o'clock and has one sharp, D major is at 2 o'clock and has two sharps, A major is at 3 o'clock and has three sharps and so on. This pattern continues all the way around until F# which has six sharps.

So, what about the flat keys on the left-hand side of the circle? The same idea applies here. Moving anti-clockwise around the circle, F major has one flat, B♭ has two flats, E♭ has three flats etc. This pattern continues all the way around until G♭, which has six flats.

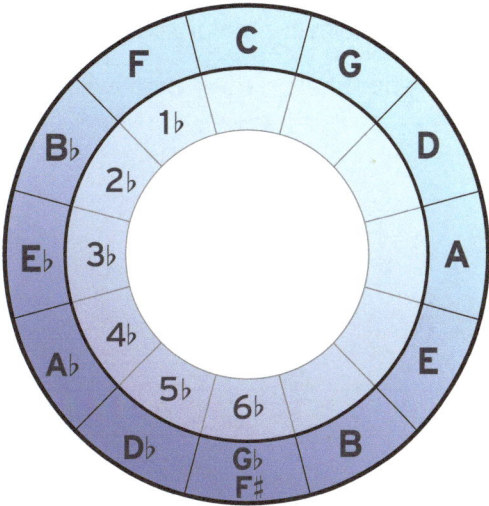

C major is the only major key that has no sharps or flats in its key signature.

Spotlight

Remember that the number of sharps or flats referrs to the accidentals that appear in that key or major scale.

For example, if we look at the left-hand side of the circle (the flat side), we can work out that E♭ has three flats. If we think of the E♭ major scale – E♭, F, G, A♭, B♭, C, D, and E♭ – we can see that those three flats are E♭, A♭, and B♭.

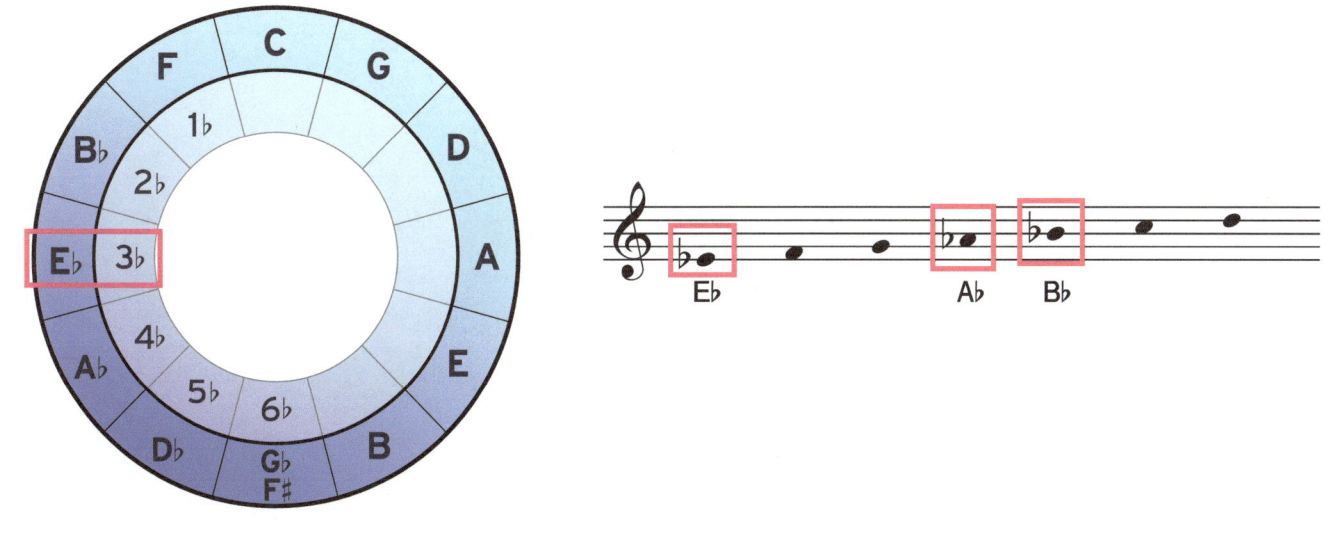

Unlike the flat side, none of the keys on the sharp side include any sharps in their actual name (apart from F♯), however, they do contain sharps within their relevant major scales.

For example, we can see that B major has five sharps. If we then work out the B major scale, we can see that those sharps are C♯, D♯, F♯, G♯, and A♯.

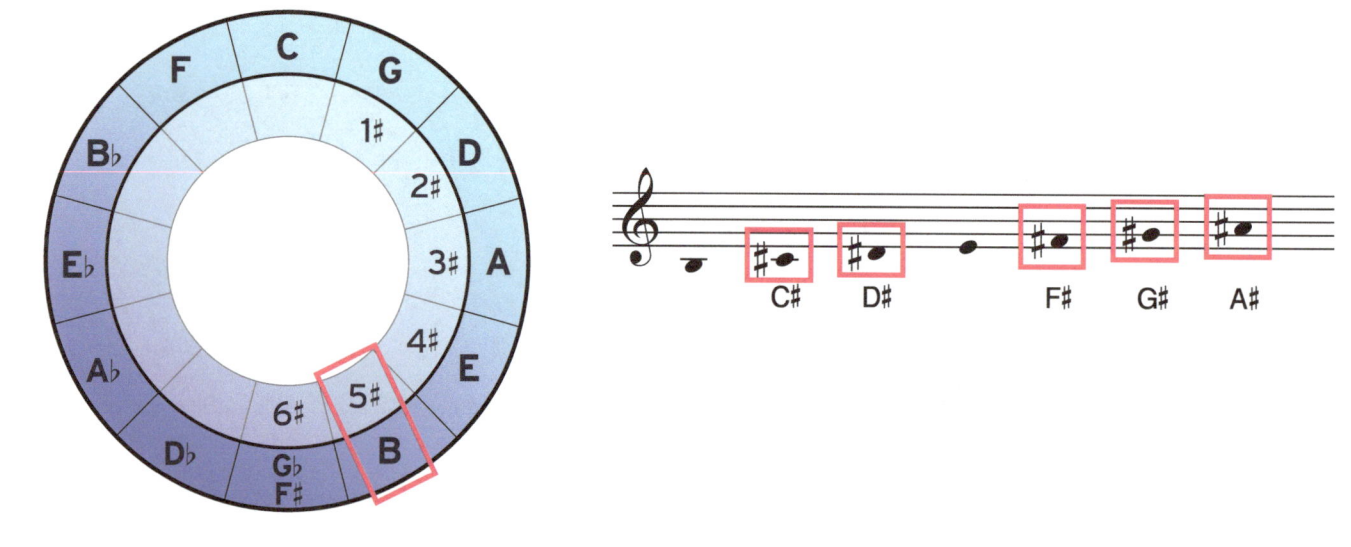

Key Signature Hand Signals

While key signatures are mainly used in notated music, in dance bands during the 1920s and 30s, if members of the band weren't sure what key a piece of music was in, rather than shouting across the stage to each other, they would hold up hand signals to indicate the key signature. This is still used in some gigs today!

If the song was in a major key, they would show the number of sharps on their hand in an upwards direction.
If a song was in a flat key, they would show the number of flats in a downward direction.

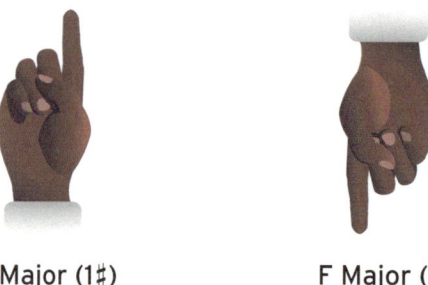

G Major (1♯)   F Major (1♭)

Musical Building Blocks

Exercise: What's the Key?

Begin by completing the circle of fifths using the blank circle below – two of the boxes have already been filled in for you.

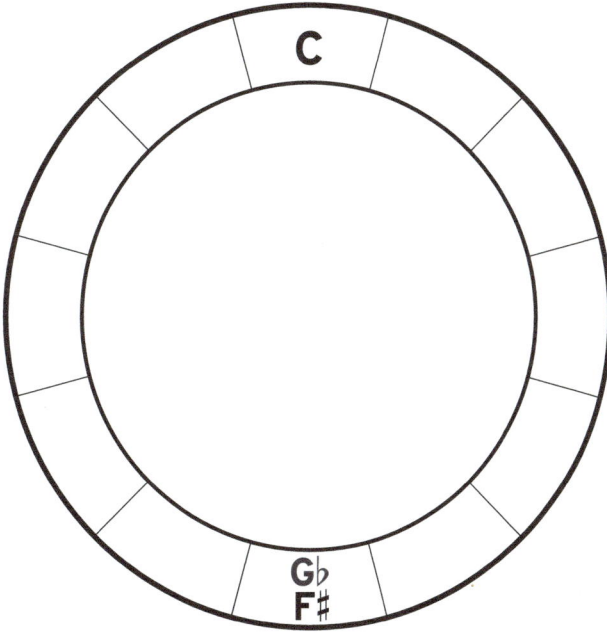

Using your completed circle of fifths, look at the following hand signs and work out the major key signatures.

Remember that if the hand sign is pointing in an upwards direction, this implies a sharp key, and a downward direction implies a flat key. The number of fingers tells you how many accidentals (sharps or flats) are in that key.

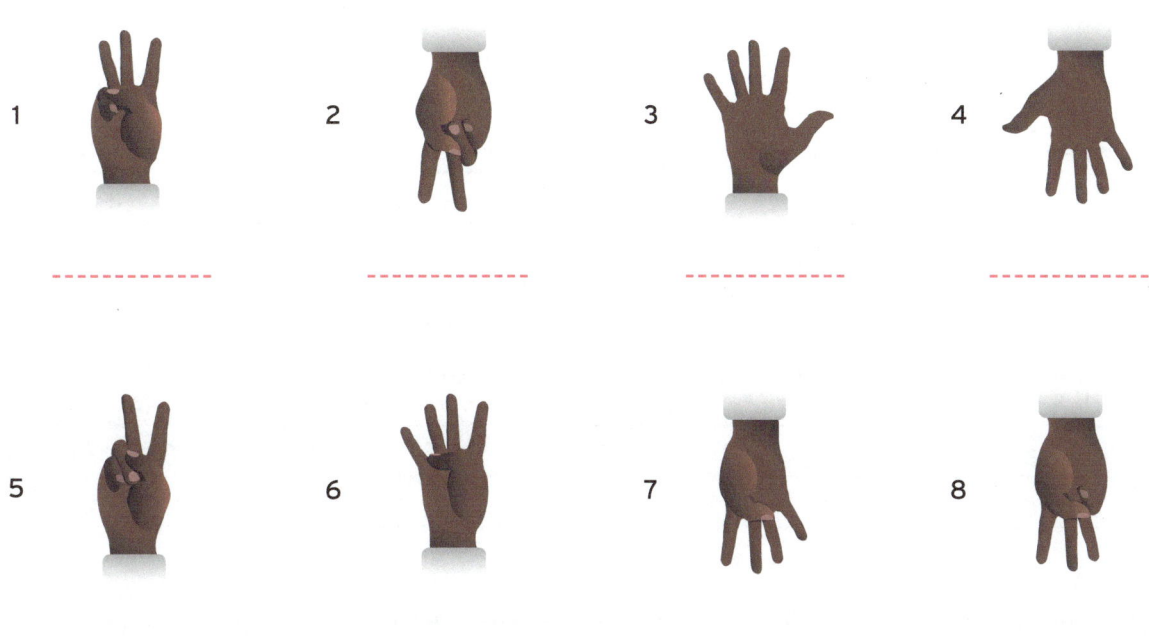

Answers can be found online, see page 8 for details.

The Order of Sharps

So how do you know which sharps or flats are in each key signature? For example, we know that G major has one sharp because it is at 1 o'clock on the circle of fifths. However, how do we know which sharp it is? Well, we could use our T-T-S-T-T-T-S formula again to work it out, however, there is a quicker way.

The order of the sharps is:

1st	2nd	3rd	4th	5th	6th	7th
F♯	C♯	G♯	D♯	A♯	E♯	B♯

If we wanted to work out which one sharp appears in the key of G major, we need to take the first sharp from the order listed above, which is F♯. Therefore, G major has one sharp, **F♯**, so the G major scale is G, A, B, C, D, E, **F♯**, G.

Let's look at another example. E major is at 4 o'clock on the circle of fifths so we know that it has four sharps. Therefore, using the order above, we take the first four sharps – **F♯**, **C♯**, **G♯**, and **D♯**. So, the notes in E major would be E, **F♯**, **G♯**, A, B, **C♯**, **D♯**, E.

We can memorise the order of sharps by using this helpful mnemonic.

Father **C**hristmas **G**ave **D**ad **A**n **E**lectric **B**lanket

Order of sharps →

You can also use the table below to help you:

Spotlight

A mnemonic is a short word or sentence where the first letters help you remember something – in this case, the order of sharps.

Major Key Signature	Number of Sharps	Sharp Notes
G major	1	F♯
D major	2	F♯, C♯
A major	3	F♯, C♯, G♯
E major	4	F♯, C♯, G♯, D♯
B major	5	F♯, C♯, G♯, D♯, A♯
F♯ major	6	F♯, C♯, G♯, D♯, A♯, E♯
C♯ major	7	F♯, C♯, G♯, D♯, A♯, E♯, B♯

Musical Building Blocks

Spotlight

You might be wondering why there are now seven sharp keys when in our original circle of fifths there were only six.

This is because it is theoretically possible to have keys with 7♯s and 7♭s. C♯ major has 7♯s and C♭ major has 7♭s. However, these are uncommon, and it's much more likely that a song will be in its enharmonic equivalent key: D♭ rather than C♯, and B rather than C♭.

Once we have understood the order of the sharps we can begin constructing a key signature. The sharps in the key signature always follow the same order, starting with F♯.

Here are the seven sharp key signatures written in the treble clef:

and the same in the bass clef:

Notice how the notes in the key signature build up cumulatively just like in the mnemonic 'Father Christmas Gave Dad An Electric Blanket'. It's also important to remember where the sharps in each key signature are placed on the stave, in both the treble and bass clefs.

Extra Info

There is a simple trick to work out the major key with a sharp key signature.

Look at the last sharp and go up a semitone. For example, the last sharp in the key signature below is C♯. Up a semitone from C♯ is D, so this key signature is a D major.

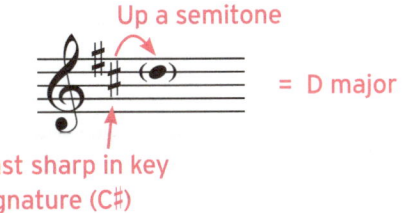

The Order of Flats

The order of flats goes in reverse to the order of sharps.

The order of flats is:

1st	2nd	3rd	4th	5th	6th	7th
B♭	E♭	A♭	D♭	G♭	C♭	F♭

If we wanted to work out which flats appear in the key of F major, we know that F major has one flat because it is one space round on the flat side of the circle (left-hand side). So, we need to take the first flat from the order: B♭. Therefore, the F major scale is F, G, A, B♭, C, D, E, F.

Let's look at another example. A♭ major has four flats because it is four sections round on the flat side of the circle. Therefore, the four flats in A♭ major are B♭, E♭, A♭, and D♭. So, the A♭ major scale is A♭, B♭, C, D♭, E♭, F, G, A♭.

The helpful mnemonic we used to remember the order of sharps was 'Father Christmas Gave Dad An Electric Blanket'. The order of flats continues the story:

Blanket **E**xplodes **A**nd **D**ad **G**ets **C**old **F**eet

→ Order of flats

Notice that this is the reverse order from the order of sharps. You can also use the table below to help you:

Major Key Signature	Number of Flats	Flat Notes
F major	1	B♭
B♭ major	2	B♭, E♭
E♭ major	3	B♭, E♭, A♭
A♭ major	4	B♭, E♭, A♭, D♭
D♭ major	5	B♭, E♭, A♭, D♭, G♭
G♭ major	6	B♭, E♭, A♭, D♭, G♭, C♭
C♭ major	7	B♭, E♭, A♭, D♭, G♭, C♭, F♭

 **Extra Info**

So we now have two ways of working out any major scale. We can use the T-T-S-T-T-T-S formula, or we can use the circle of fifths.

Musical Building Blocks

Now we have looked at the order of flats we can begin constructing the key signatures for flat keys.

Here are the seven flat key signatures written in the treble clef:

and the same in the bass clef:

Again, the flats in the key signature build up cumulatively and follow the mnemonic 'Blanket Explodes And Dad Gets Cold Feet'. Just like the sharp key signatures, it's important to remember where the flats in each key signature are placed on the stave, in both the treble and bass clefs.

 **Extra Info**

There is a simple trick to work out the major key with a flat key signature.

Look at the second to last flat. In the example below, the second to last flat in the key signature is A♭, meaning that this is A♭ major.

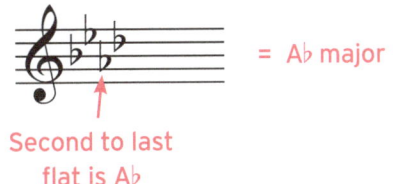 = A♭ major

Second to last flat is A♭

Unfortunately, this strategy doesn't work for F major. You'll have to remember that F major has one flat.

Exercise: What's the Key Signature?

Name the following major key signatures. Use the circle of fifths diagram to help you. Remember the sharp keys are on the right-hand side, and the flat keys are on the left-hand side of the circle.

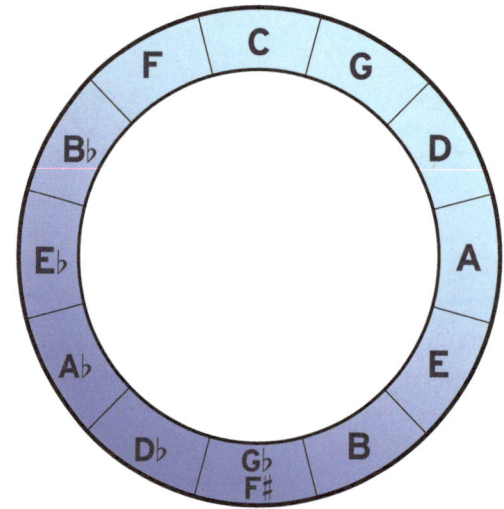

Now try writing the following key signatures on the blank staves. Make sure you consider the clef before you begin each one. Think of the mnemonic when remembering the order of the sharps and flats.

B♭ major

2. E major

G major

A♭ major

D major

6. F major

F♯ major

8. D♭ major

Answers can be found online, see page 8 for details.

Musical Building Blocks

Exercise: Adding a Key Signature

This tune includes lots of accidentals. Make it easier to read by rewriting it using the key signature of E major.

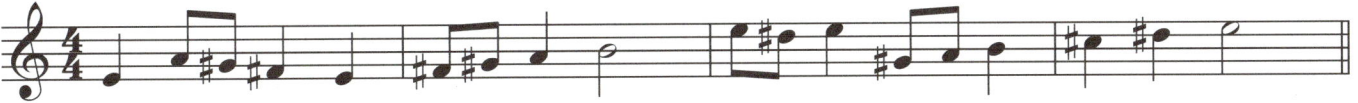

Answers can be found online, see page 8 for details.

Spotlight

At this point it would be useful to remind ourselves of the difference between a scale and a key. Keys and scales are very closely linked, and this can sometimes cause confusion.

A scale is a set of pitches that are usually played in ascending (and then descending) order.
For example, here is the F major scale ascending.

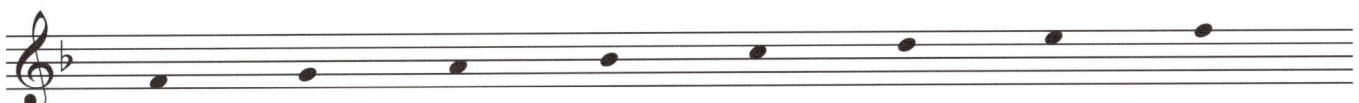

(Notice how an F major key signature has been used here, so the B on the middle line is flattened – B♭).

A key (or key centre, or tonal centre) is used when referring to a song, or section of music.
If a song is in the key of F major, then the melody might use the notes from the F major scale, but not necessarily in ascending order. For example, here is a melody in the key of F major.

Major vs Minor

So far we have only looked at major keys. However, some songs are written in a *minor key*.

Every major key has a *relative minor*, and equally, every minor key has a relative major. This is useful to know, as relative keys share the same key signature. Also, it is common for a major key to modulate (change key) to its relative minor.

Look at the following scales:

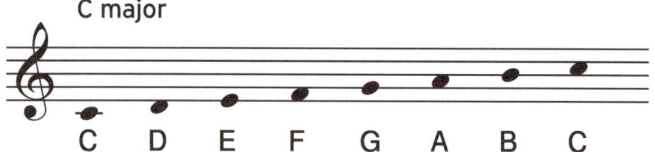 

C major and A minor are relatives because they share the same notes. The only difference is the note each scale starts on – C major starts on a C, and A natural minor starts on an A. Although these scales use the same notes overall, they sound very different when played or sung in isolation.

Listen to this track which demonstrates the C major scale ascending and descending played on the piano followed by guitar.

 2.38 C Major Scale (Piano & Guitar)

Now listen to this track which demonstrates the A natural minor scale ascending and descending.

 2.39 A Natural Minor Scale (Piano & Guitar)

Spotlight

There are other types of minor scales, however, when musicians refer to an A minor scale, they are likely talking about the natural minor scale. The natural minor scale is sometimes called the Aeolian mode.

Musical Building Blocks

Major vs Minor

Songs in a minor key have a different kind of quality from songs in a major key.

It's subjective, but minor keys have a different sound and emotional feel – sometimes people describe minor keys as sounding more solemn, sad, or ominous than music in a major key. Sometimes songwriters like to play with this idea, contrasting major keys with sad lyrics and vice versa.

Playlist: Songs in a Major Key

- George Ezra: Green Green Grass
- Kylie Minogue: I Should Be So Lucky
- Whitney Houston: I Wanna Dance with Somebody (Who Loves Me)
- The Killers: Mr. Brightside
- The Police: Every Breath You Take
- Katrina & The Waves: Walking On Sunshine
- The Beatles: Let It Be
- ABBA: Dancing Queen
- Lionel Richie: Dancing On The Ceiling

Playlist: Songs in a Minor Key

- Bill Withers: Ain't No Sunshine
- Khalid: Angels
- Billie Eilish: Billie Bossa Nova
- Britney Spears: Circus
- Ray Charles: Hit the Road Jack
- Rihanna: American Oxygen

Exercise: Working Out a Bass Line

Pick one of the songs from the playlist above and try to play or sing the bass line. First, work out the key, then find the root notes of each chord change. Work in short sections adding in any extra notes the bass may play until you can play the bass line all the way through.

This is a creative exercise, so there are no 'answers'.

Finding the Relative Minor

Here are two methods you can use to find the relative minor of a major key.

Method 1: The circle of fifths

Perhaps the easiest method is to use the circle of fifths. If we go back to visualising the circle of fifths like a clock, you can find the relative minor by going forward 15 minutes.

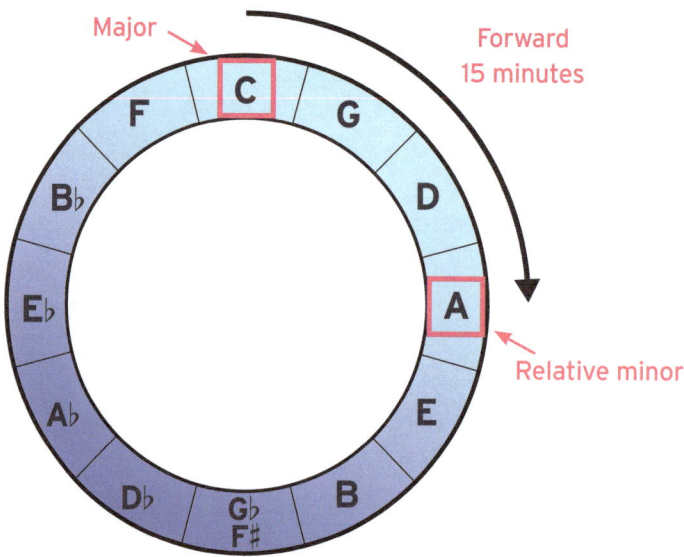

This method is also useful for finding the relative major of a minor key, in which case you do the opposite, go back 15 minutes.

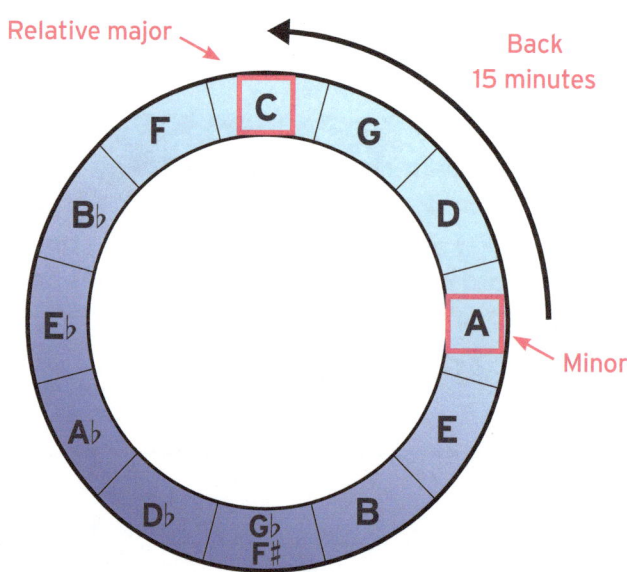

Method 2: The sixth note of the major scale

The sixth note of the major scale is the root note (1st degree) of the relative minor.

For example, take the C major scale, and then count six scale degrees (remember to include C when you count).

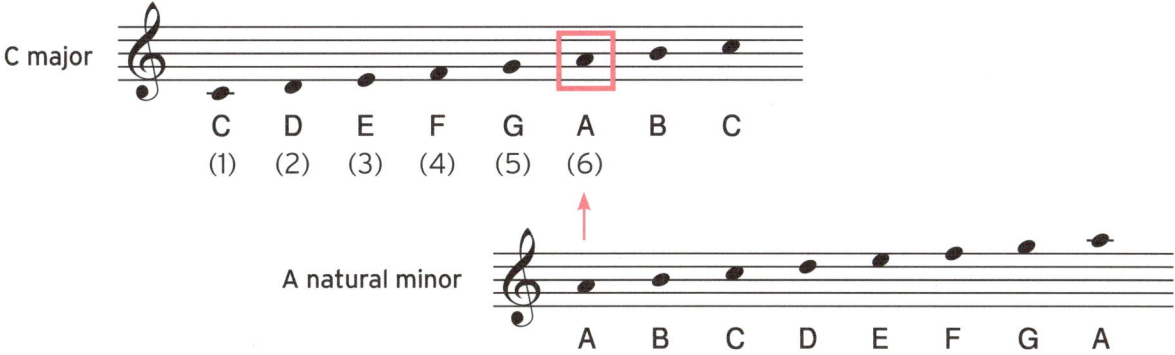

We can then construct the natural minor scale using the notes from the C major scale, but with the new starting note, in this case A.

A couple of shortcuts:

To find the relative minor on a keyboard, simply count down three semitones from your starting note (don't include the starting note when counting).

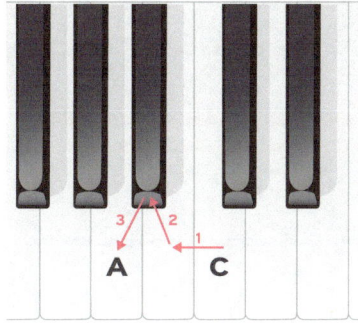

To find the relative minor on a guitar or bass, go down three frets on the same string.

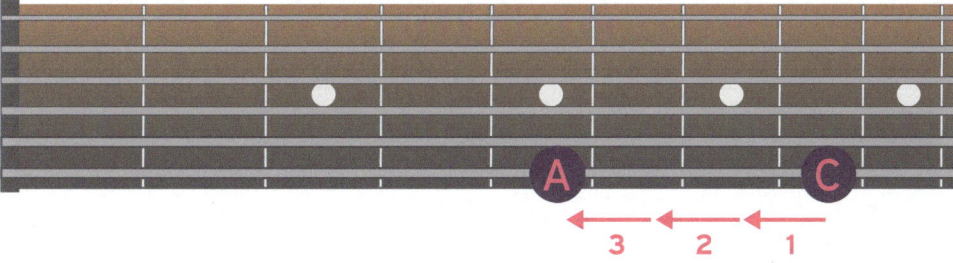

Spotlight

As you can see, there are many ways to find the same thing! Perhaps you have another way of working out the relative minor. It's about finding a strategy that works for you.

Questions

Here are some questions on the topics covered so far.

There is a Keyboard Diagram in the Appendix of this book to help you with this exercise.

1. What is the **relative minor** of **G major**? ....

2. D is the **relative major** of which minor key? ....

3. What is the **relative minor** of **B♭ major**? ....

4. E♭ is the **relative major** of which minor key? ....

5. B is the **relative minor** of which major key? ....

6. What is the **relative major** of **D minor**? ....

Answers can be found online, see page 8 for details.

Exercise: Relative Minor & Major

Exercise 1: Find the relative minor root note of the following notes.
Write the relative minor root note on the stave next to the relative major root note.

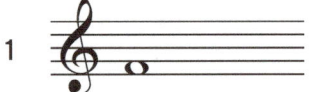 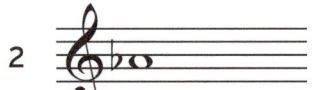 

Exercise 2: Find the relative major root note of the following notes.
Write the relative major root note on the stave next to the relative minor root note.

 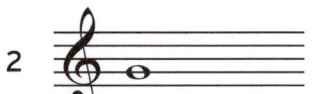 

Answers can be found online, see page 8 for details.

The Natural Minor Formula

It isn't always productive to keep thinking of a major key when talking about a minor key, so using a combination of tones (T) and semitones (S), there is a simple pattern to work out any natural minor scale, starting on any note.

Natural Minor Formula

T - S - T - T - S - T - T

Listen to this track which demonstrates the G natural minor scale, ascending and descending. Here is the G natural minor scale written in the treble clef:

 2.40 G Natural Minor Scale

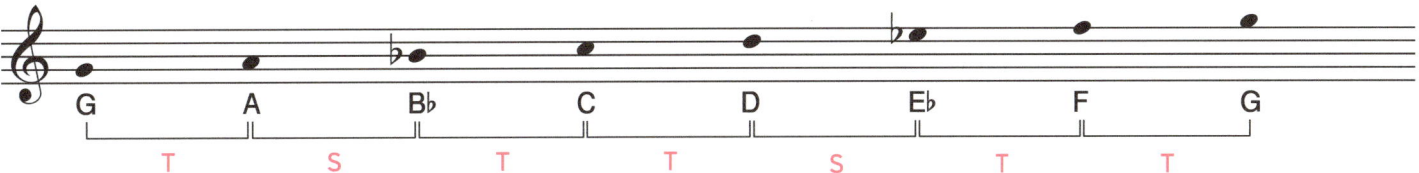

 **Spotlight**

So what is the difference between B♭ major and G minor, if they are just the same notes?

The main difference is the **tonal centre**. In other words, if the music is centred around a B♭ major progression or melody, then the key would be B♭ major. Alternatively, if the music is centred around an G minor chord progression or melody, the key would be G minor.

Extra Info

There is a helpful chart in the Appendix with every natural minor scale, written in treble and bass clef.

Exercise: Building Natural Minor Scales

Build the following natural minor scales using the formula T - S - T - T - S - T - T:

The first note for each has been provided for you.

Exercise 1 F natural minor

Exercise 2 B♭ natural minor

Exercise 3 E natural minor

Exercise 4 C natural minor

Exercise 5 B natural minor

Answers can be found online, see page 8 for details.

Minor Key Signatures

Each minor key shares the same key signature as its relative major.

For example, we know that A minor is the relative minor of C major – both these keys have no sharps or flats. Both key signatures look the same:

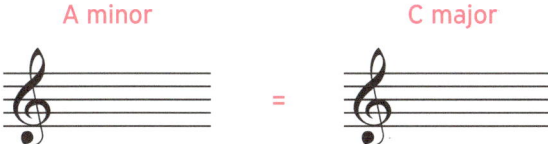

E minor is the relative minor of G major, so both use the same key signature (one sharp):

We can see that every major key has a matching minor key signature. All examples are shown in both the treble and bass clef.

Sharp Key Signatures

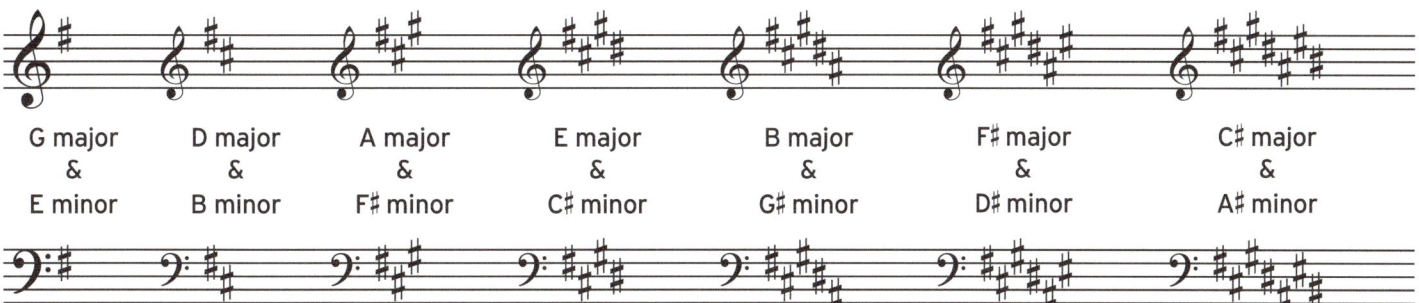

Flat Key Signatures

Here are a few rules to help us when writing these key signatures:

- Major and minor key signatures use either flats or sharps, but not both;
- The maximum number of sharps or flats in a key signature is seven;
- There is a specific order that the sharps or flats in a key signature should be written, and that never changes.

Whether you use a major or minor key signature depends on the music itself and we'll look at this in more detail in the next section.

Exercise: Write the Minor Key Signature

Write the following minor key signatures. Remember to check the clef before you begin each question.

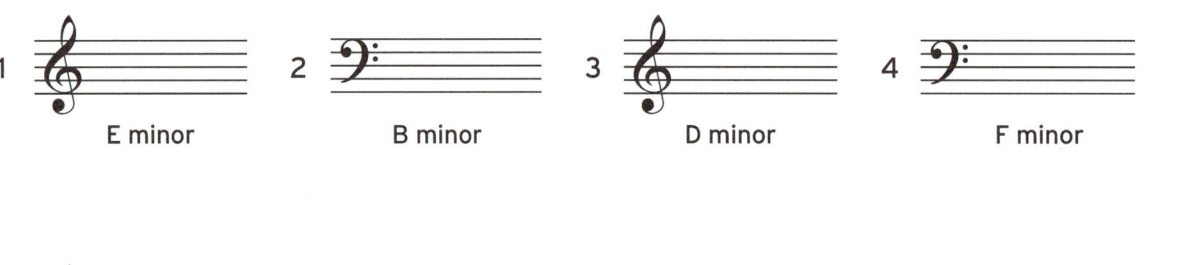

1. E minor
2. B minor
3. D minor
4. F minor

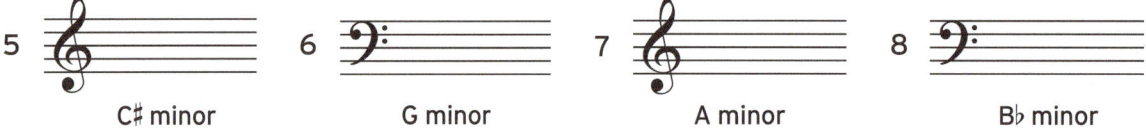

5. C♯ minor
6. G minor
7. A minor
8. B♭ minor

Answers can be found online, see page 8 for details.

Summary

There has been a lot of information in this section. However, by far the most important topic covered is the major scale. The rest of this book is going to focus on elements of harmony that all relate to the major scale.

The best piece of advice I could give anyone is to **internalise** all the major scales. Learn how to sing them, play them, and memorise all the note names. This will be an incredibly productive use of your time.

I often get asked why it's important to learn these major scales and, going forward, the major scales form the basis of so much – scales, chords, keys, and much more.

It's also about your speed of thought. Imagine if every time you wanted to write a sentence you had to use the dictionary to look up each word. It would take a long time! While the major scale formula (T-T-S-T-T-T-S) is a great starting point, I'd advise moving away from this as quickly as possible. It isn't always practical to go through that formula every time you need to work something out.

All the major scales are listed in the Appendix at the back of this book so dedicate time to memorising them – you certainly won't regret it! At first you may have to work out the patterns in your head, but after some time writing and playing with the concepts they will become automatic.

Harmony

Triads

A chord is when multiple notes (typically three) are played at the same time. There are many different types of chord, but we are going to begin by looking at the most common type of chord – the triad.

A triad is when three notes are played at the same time (derived from 'tri' – meaning three).

Major Triads

To build a major triad, we need to know the first five notes of a major scale. For example, if we want to build a G major triad, the first five notes of G major are G, A, B, C, and D. There is a diagram in the Appendix, displaying every major scale in the treble and bass clef.

A major triad consists of the 1st, 3rd, and 5th degrees of the major scale. For example, a G major triad consists of the notes G, B, and D. The 1st degree of the scale is often referred to as the root of the chord.

Listen to this track which demonstrates a G major triad being played on a piano. First it is played arpeggiated (each note is played ascending), then as a block (all three notes together).

 3.01 G Major Triad

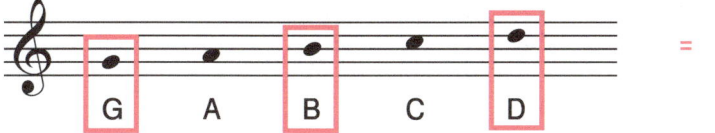

In terms of intervals, a major triad consists of a major 3rd with a minor 3rd on top. For example, in the context of G major, G-B is a major 3rd and B-D is a minor 3rd.

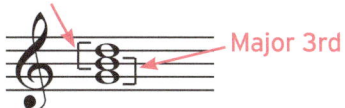

Chord Symbols

Chord symbols are an easy way of describing the notes in a chord. You'll find them in many forms of notation including chord charts, lead sheets, piano/vocal/guitar arrangements, and improvised sections etc.

The chord symbol for a major triad uses the root of the triad as a capital letter, eg, G (we don't need to write the word 'major' afterwards).

Let's try building another major triad, this time on B♭. We know that the first five notes of B♭ major are B♭, C, D, E♭, and F. A triad is made up of the root, the 3rd, and the 5th, therefore a B♭ major triad consists of B♭, D, and F. The chord symbol for a B♭ major triad is simply B♭.

Listen to this track which demonstrates this B♭ major triad being played on a piano. It is first arpeggiated (each note is played ascending), then played as a block (all three notes together).

 3.02 B♭ Major Triad

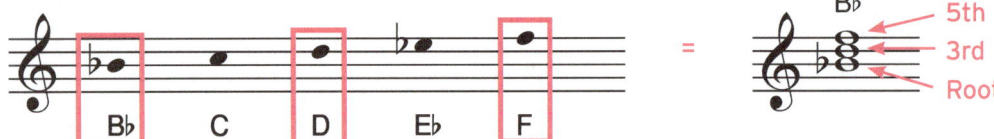

Exercise: Major Triads

Exercise 1: Using the chord symbol, identify and fill in the missing note from the major triad. Make sure to determine whether the missing note is the root, 3rd, or 5th. Make sure you check the clef before you begin.

 3.03 Major Triads Ex. 1

To help you connect the sounds of these triads with the notation, listen to this track which demonstrates these major triads played on a piano. Try to hear the notes in your head as you read them on the page. You might need your instrument to help you. Each triad is arpeggiated, then played as a block.

Exercise 2: Build the following major triads. Begin by working out the first five notes in the relevant major scale, then take the root, the 3rd, and the 5th, and stack them on top of each other.

 3.04 Major Triads Ex. 2

To help you connect the sounds of these triads with the notation, listen to this track which demonstrates these major triads played on a piano.

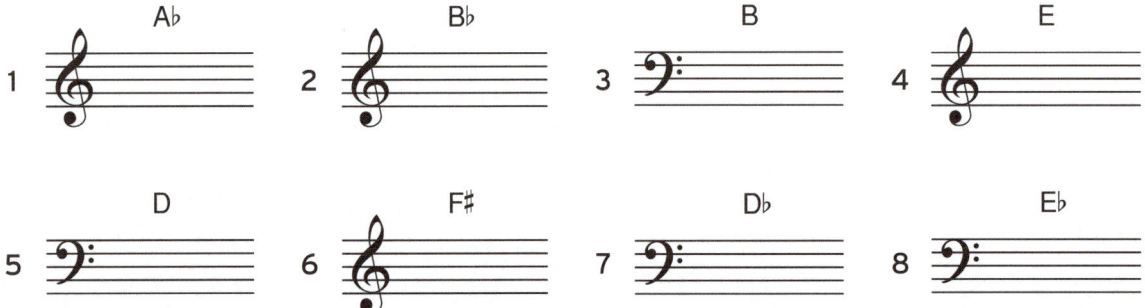

Answers can be found online, see page 8 for details.

Harmony

Minor Triads

Minor triads also consist of the 1st, 3rd, and 5th degrees of the relevant major scale, however, the 3rd is flattened/lowered by a semitone (♭3).

So, for example, a G minor triad would consist of G, B♭ and D. The chord symbol for a minor triad uses the root of the triad as a capital letter followed by a small 'm', eg, **Gm**.

Listen to this track which demonstrates this G minor triad being played on a piano. It is first arpeggiated (each note is played ascending), then played as a block (all three notes together).

 3.05 G Minor Triad

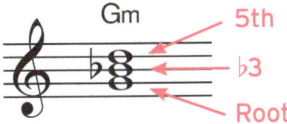

In terms of intervals, a minor triad consists of a minor 3rd with a major 3rd on top. For example, in the context of G minor (G-B♭ is a minor 3rd, and B♭-D is a major 3rd).

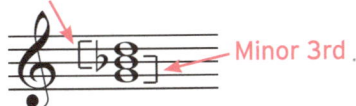

 **Spotlight**

Sometimes, musicians write a small dash, eg, G- , to represent a minor triad. However, this can often be difficult to read in certain fonts. A small 'm' is usually clearer.

 **Extra Info**

The intervals in a major triad are reversed in a minor triad.

Major triads are made up of a major 3rd with a minor 3rd on top.
Minor triads are made up of a minor 3rd with a major 3rd on top.

MAJOR TRIAD	MINOR TRIAD
Minor 3rd	Major 3rd
+	+
Major 3rd	Minor 3rd

Spotlight

You could also find a G minor triad by taking the first five notes of G natural minor (G, A, B♭, C, and D) and then taking the root, the 3rd, and the 5th. However, going forward, it's a useful system to be able to work out all the chords in relation to the major scale.

Let's go through the same process for B♭ minor. We know that a B♭ major triad is made up of B♭, D, and F so to get B♭ minor, we need to flatten the 3rd. This means that the D becomes a D♭.

Listen to this track which demonstrates this B♭ minor triad being played on a piano. It is first arpeggiated, then played as a block.

 3.06 B♭ Minor Triad

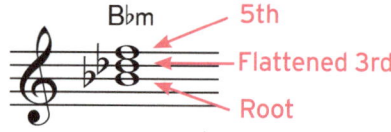

Harmony

Exercise: Minor Triads

Exercise 1
Using the chord symbol, identify and fill in the missing note from the minor triad. Make sure to determine whether the missing note is the root, 3rd, or 5th. Make sure you check the clef before you begin.

 3.07 Minor Triads Ex. 1

To help you connect the sounds of these triads with the notation, listen to this track which demonstrates these minor triads played on a piano. Try to hear the notes in your head as you read them on the page. You might need your instrument to help you. Each triad is arpeggiated, then played as a block.

Exercise 2
Build the following minor triads. Make sure you check the clef before you begin. Note that if you need to flatten a note that is a sharp, it becomes a natural.

 3.08 Minor Triads Ex. 2

To help you connect the sounds of these triads with the notation, listen to this track which demonstrates these minor triads played on a piano. Each triad is arpeggiated, then played as a block twice.

Answers can be found online, see page 8 for details.

Major and minor triads form the basis of many chord progressions, and it is important to be able to aurally recognise the difference between them.

Remember the only difference between a major triad and a minor triad is the 3rd. The 3rd of a major triad is major, and the 3rd of a minor triad is minor.

Exercise: Major or Minor Triad?

Listen to the following tracks and identify whether the triads being played are major or minor. Listen carefully to the 3rd. Is it a major 3rd or a minor 3rd?

Each triad will be arpeggiated and then played as a block chord twice.

🔊 3.09 Major or Minor Triad? Ex. 1 ....

🔊 3.10 Major or Minor Triad? Ex. 2 ....

🔊 3.11 Major or Minor Triad? Ex. 3 ....

🔊 3.12 Major or Minor Triad? Ex. 4 ....

🔊 3.13 Major or Minor Triad? Ex. 5 ....

🔊 3.14 Major or Minor Triad? Ex. 6 ....

Answers can be found online, see page 8 for details.

Sus2 and Sus4 Triads

The word sus (short for suspended) implies that the 3rd of the chord is replaced with another note, either the 2nd or the 4th degree of the scale.

Sus2

Sus2 means the 3rd of the chord is replaced with the 2nd. To work out the notes in a sus2 triad we need to take the root, the 2nd, and the 5th of the relevant major scale. For example, G(sus2) would be G, A, and D.

Listen to this track which demonstrates this G(sus2) triad being played on a piano. It is first arpeggiated, then played as a block.

 3.15 Gsus2 Triad

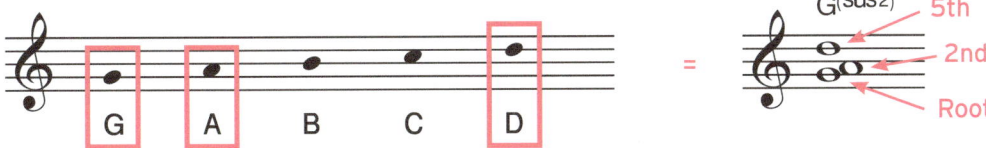

In terms of intervals, sus2 triads are made up of a major 2nd, with a perfect 4th on top.

Sus4

Sus4 means that the 3rd of the chord is replaced with the 4th. To work out the notes in a sus4 triad we need to take the root, the 4th, and the 5th of the relevant major scale. For example, G(sus4) would be G, C, and D.

Listen to this track which demonstrates this G(sus4) triad being played on a piano. It is first arpeggiated, then played as a block.

 3.16 Gsus4 Triad

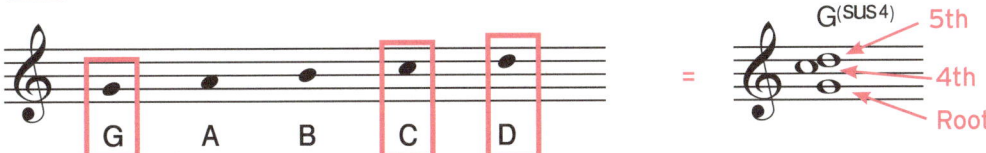

In terms of intervals, sus4 triads are made up of a perfect 4th, with a major 2nd on top.

Sus2 and Sus4 are not major or minor chords as there is no 3rd. This gives them a slightly ambiguous quality.

Remember it is the middle note in the triad that makes the difference between sus2 and sus4. If the triad is sus2 then it contains the 2nd degree of the major scale. If the triad is sus4 then it contains the 4th degree of the major scale.

Sus4 chords often resolve to a major triad of the same letter name, ie, F(sus4) – F. This is because the 4th note of the sus4 chord is a semitone away from the 3rd of the major triad. This creates a sense of tension and resolution as the 4th note resolves down to the 3rd note.

Extra Info

The intervals when building a sus2 are reversed in a sus4 triad.

Sus2 triads are made up of a major 2nd, with a perfect 4th on top.
Sus4 triads are made up of a perfect 4th, with a major 2nd on top.

SUS2	SUS4
Perfect 4th	Major 2nd
+	+
Major 2nd	Perfect 4th

Exercise: Sus2 or Sus4?

Build the following sus2 and sus4 triads. Make sure you check the clef before you begin.

Begin by working out the first five notes in the relevant major scale. If you are building a sus2 triad, take the root, the 2nd, and the 5th and stack them on top of each other. If you are building a sus4 triad, take the root, the 4th, and the 5th and stack them on top of each other.

 3.17 Building Sus Chords

To help you connect the sounds of these intervals with the notation, listen to this track which demonstrates these triads played on a piano. Each triad is arpeggiated, then played as a block twice.

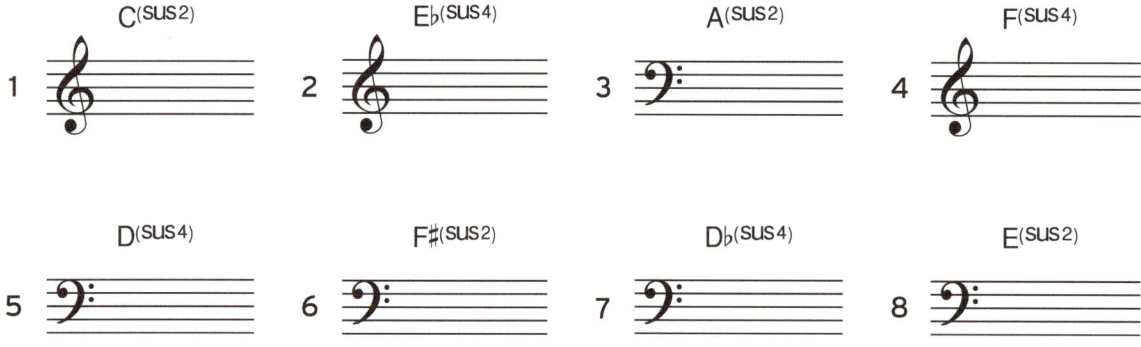

Answers can be found online, see page 8 for details.

Harmony

Exercise: Sus2 or Sus4?

Identify whether the triads are sus2 or sus4. Listen carefully to the middle note. Is it a 2nd (sus2) or 4th (sus4)?

Each triad will be arpeggiated and then played as a block chord twice.

🔊 3.18 Sus2 or Sus4? Ex. 1 ....

🔊 3.19 Sus2 or Sus4? Ex. 2 ....

🔊 3.20 Sus2 or Sus4? Ex. 3 ....

🔊 3.21 Sus2 or Sus4? Ex. 4 ....

🔊 3.22 Sus2 or Sus4? Ex. 5 ....

🔊 3.23 Sus2 or Sus4? Ex. 6 ....

Answers can be found online, see page 8 for details.

Summary

So far, we have looked at four different types of triads – major, minor, sus2, and sus4. The only difference between all these triads is the middle note.

C(sus2) = 5th / **2nd** / Root

Cm = 5th / **Flattened 3rd** / Root

C = 5th / **3rd** / Root

C(sus4) = 5th / **4th** / Root

Triads Within a Major Key

As we've established, a key is the main group of notes that form the basis of a piece of music. Usually, these notes are from a particular scale. For example, if a song is in the key of C major, most of the notes in the melody, bass line, and chords will usually be from the C major scale.

Within each major key, there are a set of diatonic chords that can be created. Diatonic means 'within the notes of the key'.

Let's go back to the C major scale:

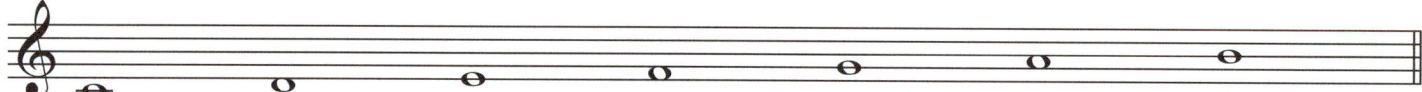

Diatonic Chords

Using the notes in the C major scale, we can build a series of triads on each degree. The chord symbols for each triad are written above. Listen to this track which demonstrates these triads being played on a piano.

 3.24 Triads in C

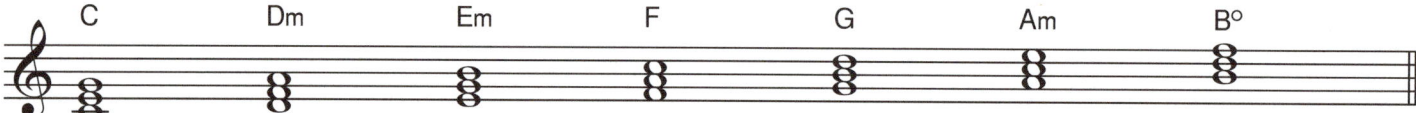

Within C major, we can see that there are **three major triads** (C, F, and G) and **three minor triads** (Dm, Em, and Am).

Roman Numerals

As well as using chord symbols, we can also analyse each of these triads using Roman numerals.

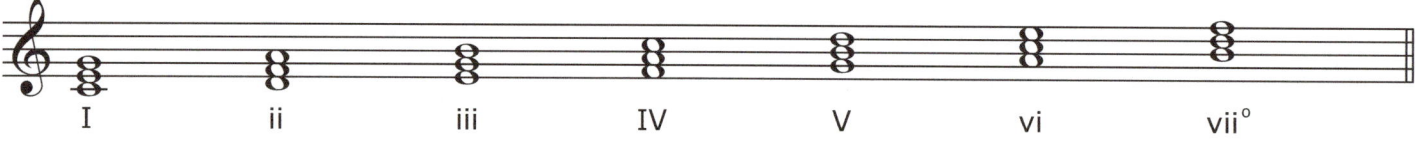

Roman numerals are often used when describing harmony so it is a good idea to become familiar with this system as it will allow you to analyse chord progressions in any key.

Spotlight

The triad built on the B (the 7th degree of the major scale) has a little circle next to it. We haven't looked at this type of triad yet, however, this is known as a diminished triad.

Diminished triads are made up of the root, a flattened 3rd, and a flattened 5th. These are explored fully in volume 2. For the moment, we're going to focus on the major and minor triads within a key.

Harmony

Spotlight

If Roman numerals are unfamiliar to you, there are two main symbols you need to know. I, which is the symbol for 1, and V, which is the symbol for 5.

- The numbers 1, 2, and 3 are self-explanatory — I, II, and III
- 4 is written as IV (with an I to the left of the V to imply that this is subtracted from the V)
- 6 and 7 are written an I to the right of the V, to imply that these are added on

When analysing harmony, if a Roman numeral is a capital, this means that the chord is major, and if it is lowercase then this implies a minor chord. For example, in the key of C major, chord I is C major, so it has an uppercase Roman numeral. Chord ii is D minor, so a lowercase Roman numeral is used.

In the key of C major, we now have six chords (triads) available to us (we are still ignoring chord vii, for now!).

If we were planning on writing a song in the key of C major, these chords would be a strong place to start.

The following diagram displays these chords — the three major triads (C, F, and G) are at the top, with the three minor triads (Dm, Em and Am) below. The major triads on the top are referred to as primary triads, and the minor triads below are secondary triads.

Key of C Major

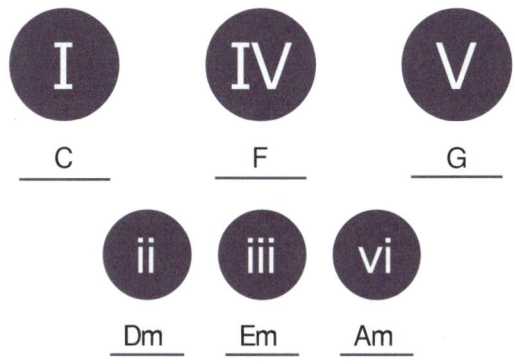

Exercise: Chords Within a Key

Complete the following diagrams. Begin by working out the major scales for the keys listed. Write the chords on the lines provided.

Exercise 1: F major

------- ------- -------

------- ------- -------

Exercise 2: G major

------- ------- -------

------- ------- -------

Exercise 3: B♭ major

------- ------- -------

------- ------- -------

Answers can be found online, see page 8 for details.

Chord Progressions

A chord progression is the order of chords that make up a piece of music. When a chord changes, it provides harmonic movement underneath the melody and lyrics. This changes the colour, atmosphere, and direction of the music. Sometimes you'll hear musicians referring to the chord progression of a piece of music as the harmony or changes.

Here is an example of a chord sequence in the key of C. This sequence uses all the diatonic major, and minor triads. Listen to this track of the progression played by a band (drums, bass, keys, and guitar).

 3.25 Chord Sequence in C (All Major and Minor Triads)

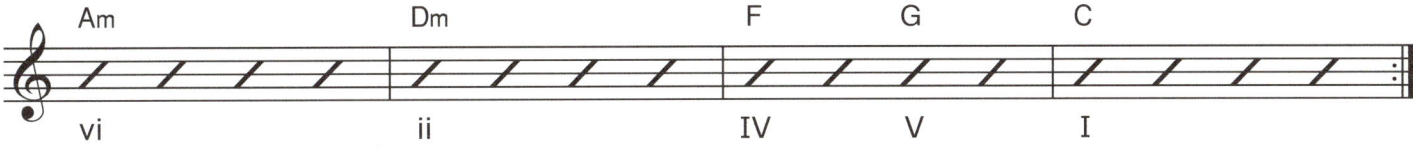

As performers and songwriters, it is useful to understand how chord sequences are constructed. Knowing how chords relate to each other will make your progressions strong, natural, and memorable. While some interesting chord changes can be created by experimenting with random chords, many songs follow formulaic patterns.

Not only do we need to understand the theory behind these sequences, but we also need to be able to recognise them by ear. This next section will go through some of the most common chord changes within a key.

Chord I

Some songs only contain the triad built on the tonic: chord I. For example, if the music is in C major, the harmony would stay on a C triad. It is rare to find songs that only use one chord, however, they tend to have a bluesy feel and are sometimes built around a riff (a repetitive musical pattern).

Listen to this track which shows the following chord progression played by a band. The 8-bar sequence is played twice. The chord symbol is above the stave, and the Roman numeral below. The four slashes in each bar represent the main pulse beats.

 3.26 Chord Sequence – Chord I

Although we are calling this a chord 'progression', this sequence only contains one chord. Most chord progressions usually contain more than one chord. While listening to the track, notice how the chords don't seem to move anywhere – the harmony remains static.

 Repeat end sign

The notation below includes a *repeat end sign*, at the end of the eighth bar. This means that the sequence is repeated, so it will now be sixteen bars long (two lots of eight bars).

If the repeat sign were to appear at the end of four bars, then the chord sequence would be eight bars long (two lots of four bars).

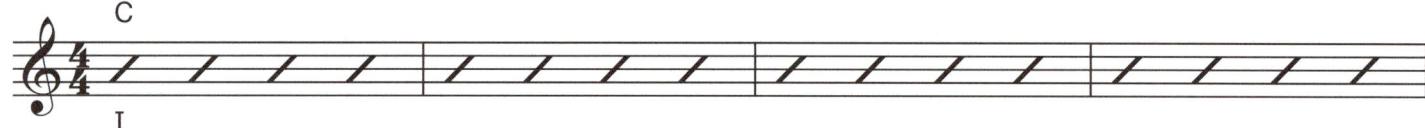

Spotlight

Notice when writing chord progressions you don't need to restate the chord symbol in each bar, only if the chord changes. In the example above, the whole eight bars remain on chord I, so this is stated at the beginning and doesn't need to be repeated as the chord doesn't change.

Playlist: Chord I

The songs in this Spotify Playlist all stay on chord I. Note that some of the songs are not in the key of C major, however, if they were transposed into the key of C, the main chord would be C major.

- Sonny & Cher: The Beat Goes On
- Lucinda Williams: Joy
- Sly & The Family Stone: Thank You (Falettinme Be Mice Elf Agin)

Harmony

Chords I & V

If a song moves between chords I and V, then the progression is moving between the tonic and the dominant. In the key of C, the chords would be C and G.

Chord I can sound like 'home' because it's often the starting point and resting place, giving a sense of stability and resolution. Chord V, can sound like it's 'leading away' from home due to its tension and desire to resolve back to chord I, creating a sense of movement and anticipation.

Listen to this track which features the band playing the following chord progression which exclusively uses chords I and V.

 3.27 Chord Sequence – Chords I & V

In this example, the chords are changing every bar. Listen to how the second bar has a different sound from the first bar and so on. The chord progression is taking us on a journey.

If you are struggling to hear the chord change, listen to this track which contains just the bass and drums. The bass player is playing the root of each chord – a C on chord I and a G on chord V.

 3.28 Chord Sequence – Chords I & V (Bass & Drums)

When identifying chord progressions by ear, it can really help to initially listen to the bass line as this can help us work out the root movement, which can in turn help us to identify the chords being used. Try learning to sing the bass line along with the track. This will help get your ears accustomed to that I-V movement.

Notice how the chords move more quickly in the seventh bar of the sequence; rather than each chord lasting for four beats, the chords only last for two beats each. The pacing of chords in a sequence is called harmonic rhythm, so the harmonic rhythm is faster in the seventh bar than in the rest of the sequence.

Playlist: Chords I and V

The songs in this Spotify Playlist mainly use chords I and V.

Note that some of the songs are not in the key of C major, however, if the songs were transposed into the key of C, the main chords would be C and G.

- Billy Ray Cyrus: Achy Breaky Heart
- The Dixie Cups: Iko Iko
- Bruce Springsteen: Pay Me My Money Down

Exercise: Hear the Changes (Part 1)

Listen to each track which contains a chord progression played by a band. The chord progression only includes chords I and V and all the progressions begin on chord I.

Write in the Roman numerals and the chord symbols. The key signature and the time signature have been provided for you.

If you are struggling to keep track of where the chords are changing, put a small star above the stave wherever you hear a chord change. After doing this, go back and see if you can work out whether it is chord I or V. You could use an instrument to help you, or you could sing the bass line along with the sequence. Once you have done this, work out the names of the chord symbols that fit with the Roman numerals.

The key chord is sounded before the count-in to give you a sense of the key.

Exercise 1 (4 bars) F major (chords I and V)

 3.29 Hear the Changes (Part 1) Ex. 1

Exercise 2 (4 bars) G major (chords I and V). Remember to check the time signature!

 3.30 Hear the Changes (Part 1) Ex. 2

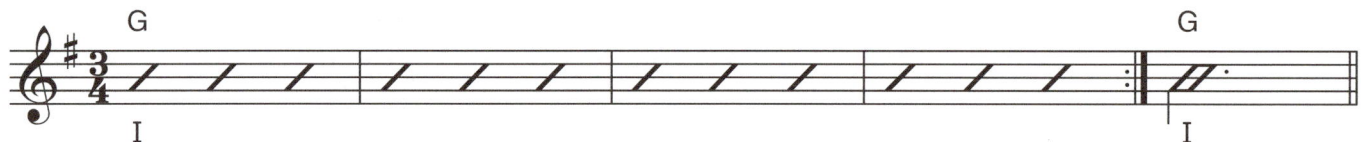

Exercise 3 (8 bars) B♭ major (chords I and V). Some bars have more than one chord in them!

 3.31 Hear the Changes (Part 1) Ex. 3

Answers can be found online, see page 8 for details.

Cadences

There are other ways we can describe the movements within a chord progression. Cadences are like punctuation marks in a sentence and can help us understand the structure of a piece of music. Cadences can signal to our ears that a musical phrase or section is coming to an end, they can create a sense of resolution or tension. Cadences are a shorthand for describing a chord movement. The term comes from the Latin word *cadere* which means 'to fall'.

Perfect Cadence

A perfect cadence is when chord V moves to chord I. In other words, the V chord (dominant) falls to the I chord (tonic) creating a sense of resolution. A perfect cadence in music is like a full stop and can mark the end of a musical phrase, giving a sense of closure and finality to the music, just as a full stop ends a sentence.

While perfect cadences are often found at the ends of sections, phrases, or songs, they can also appear anywhere the songwriter chooses.

In the key of C, a perfect cadence would be G (V) resolving to C (I).

Listen to this track which demonstrates an example of a perfect cadence played on the piano followed by guitar.

 3.32 Perfect Cadence (Piano & Guitar)

Perfect Cadence

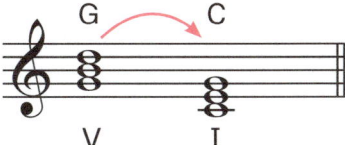

Imperfect Cadence

Chord I moving to chord V is an example of an imperfect cadence. An imperfect cadence is like a comma because it creates a momentary pause or interruption in the musical flow, similar to how a comma indicates a brief pause in a sentence without concluding it. An imperfect cadence leaves the listener expecting more, just as a comma leaves a reader anticipating the continuation of the thought in a sentence.

These cadences can sound unresolved or unfinished. It would be unusual to find an imperfect cadence at the end of a song, but an imperfect cadence could be found just before the end of a section or phrase.

In the key of C, an imperfect cadence would be C (I) moving to G (V).

Listen to this track which demonstrates an example of an imperfect cadence played on the piano followed by guitar.

 3.33 Imperfect Cadence (Piano & Guitar)

Imperfect Cadence

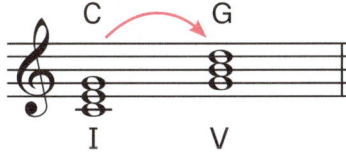

Spotlight

Imperfect cadences aren't exclusively I-V. They can be any progression that ends on a V chord. For example, another imperfect cadence could be ii-V or IV-V.

In the following chord progression we can see that the entire sequence features exclusively perfect and imperfect cadences.

Listen to this track which demonstrates this chord sequence played by a band.

 3.34 Chord Sequence – Imperfect & Perfect Cadences

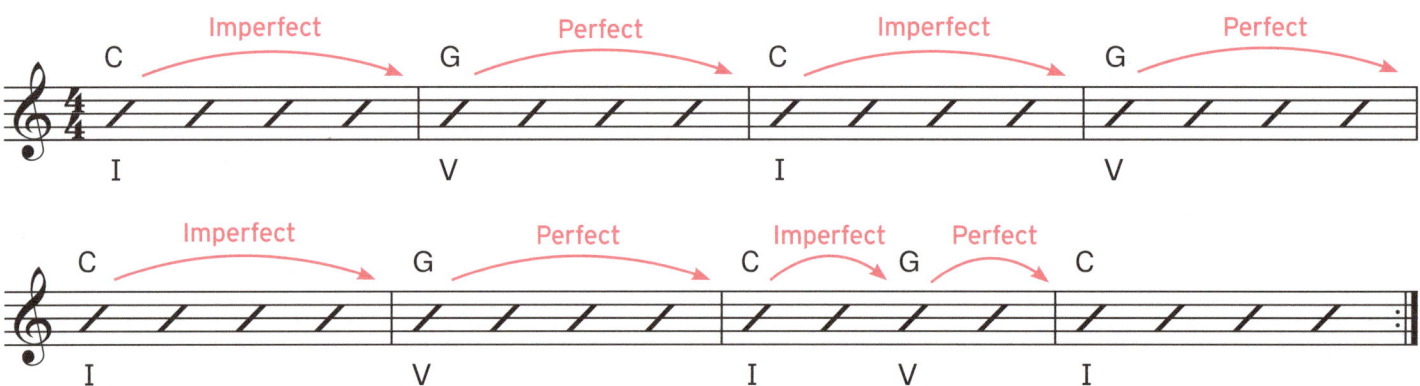

While it is useful to understand cadences, these labels are more relevant when analysing Western Classical music. Perfect and imperfect cadences in closely related keys formed a significant part of the harmonic vocabulary of the Classical period

In popular music, the term 'cadence' is less widely used, and many musicians will tend to refer to a perfect cadence as a V–I progression. Having said this, being able to recognise these common chord progressions aurally is a very useful skill.

Chords I & IV

Another important movement is between chords I and IV. For example, in the key of C, the progression would move between C (tonic) and F (subdominant).

Listen to this track which features the band playing the following chord progression which exclusively uses chords I and IV.

 3.35 Chord Sequence – Chords I & IV

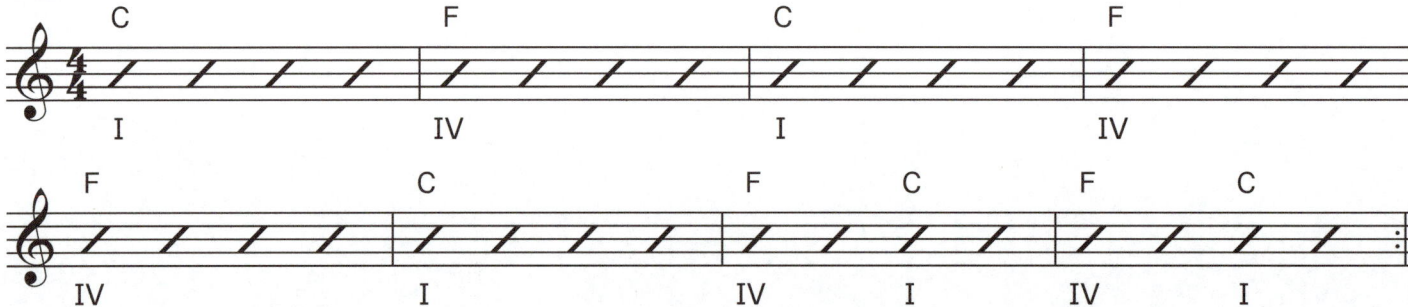

Harmony

Again, if you are struggling to hear the chord change, listen to this track which just contains the bass and drums.

 3.36 Chord Sequence – Chords I & IV (Bass & Drums)

Listen specifically to the bass playing the root of each chord – a C on chord I and an F on chord IV. It's subjective, but chord IV is sometimes considered to be a 'warm' sound. Be sure to sing and play these progressions to get a sense of how they sound and feel.

Plagal Cadence

A *plagal* cadence is when chord IV moves to chord I. This is sometimes referred to as the 'Amen Cadence' because it can be found at the end of many church hymns with the 'Ah' on chord IV and 'men' on chord I.

Listen to this track which demonstrates an example of a plagal cadence played on the piano followed by guitar.

 3.37 Plagal Cadence (Piano & Guitar)

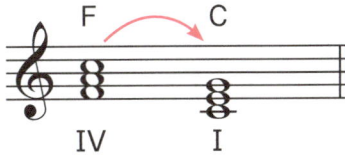

Going back to the chord progression we can see that the sequence features several plagal cadences.

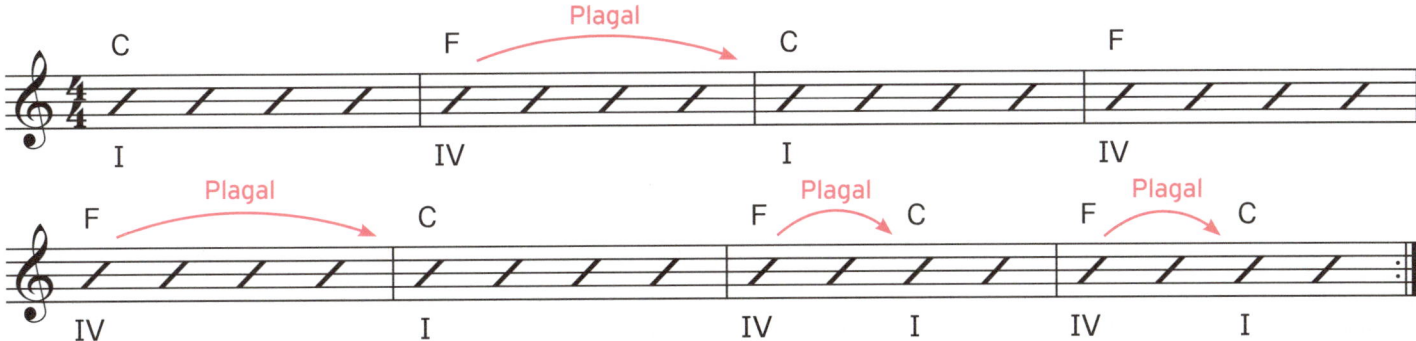

As well as writing chord symbols, we can also notate the triads.

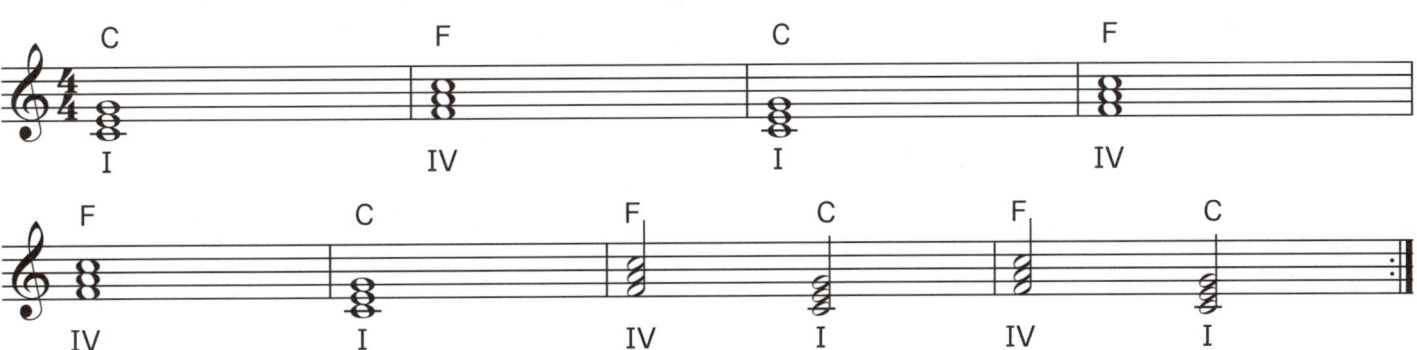

Playlist: Chords I and IV

The songs in this Spotify Playlist mainly use chords I and IV

Note that some of the songs in this playlist are not in the key of C major, however, if the songs were transposed into the key of C, the main chords would be C and F.

- Joe Cocker: Feelin' Alright
- Bruce Springsteen: Born in the U.S.A.
- The Staple Singers: I'll Take You There

Exercise: Hear the Changes (Part 2)

Listen to each track which contains a chord progression played by a band. The chord progression only includes chords I and IV and all the progressions begin on chord I.

Write in the Roman numerals and the chord symbols. The key signatures and time signatures have been provided for you.

The key chord is sounded before the count-in to give you a sense of the key.

Exercise 1 (4 bars) D major (chords I and IV). Some bars have more than one chord in them!

 3.38 Hear the Changes (Part 2) Ex. 1

Exercise 2 (4 bars) F major (chords I and IV). Some bars have more than one chord in them!

 3.39 Hear the Changes (Part 2) Ex. 2

Harmony

> **Exercise 3 (8 bars) B♭ major (chords I and IV)**
>
> In addition to writing the Roman numerals and chord symbols, notate the triads on the stave.
>
>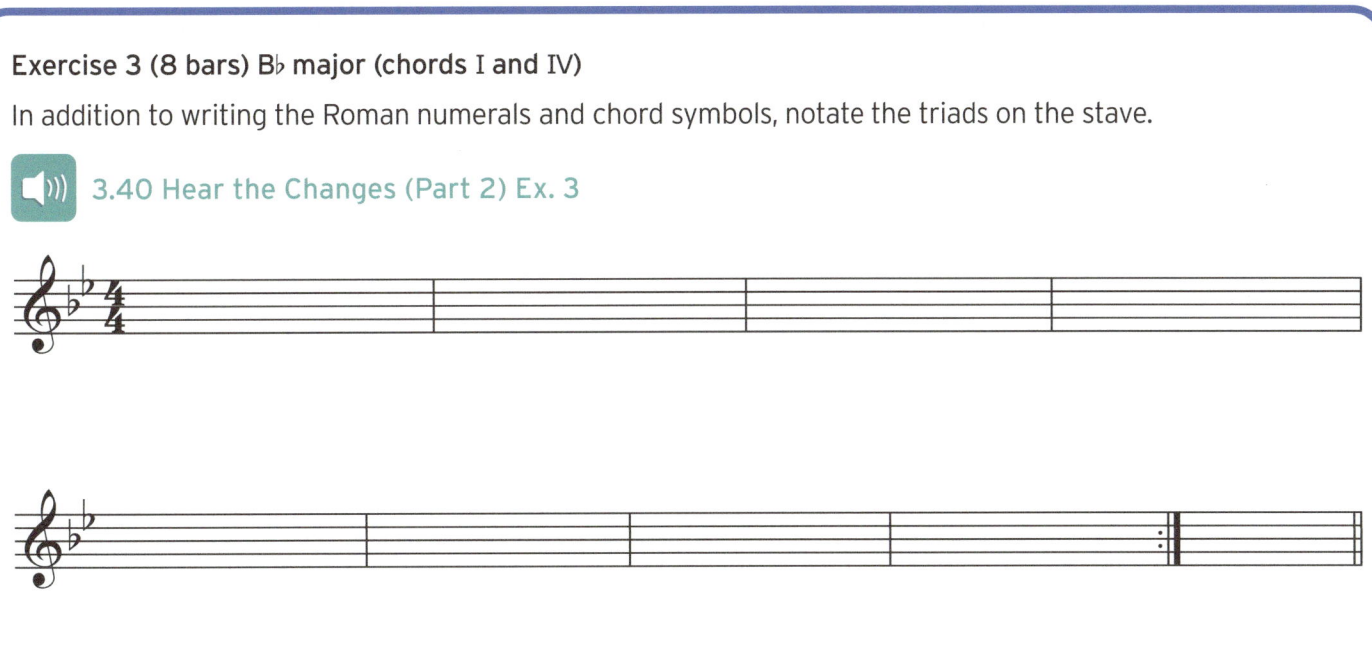
> 3.40 Hear the Changes (Part 2) Ex. 3
>
> Answers can be found online, see page 8 for details.

Chords I, IV & V

Chords I, IV, and V form the basis of many songs. Here is an example of a chord sequence that uses these three chords in the key of C major (C, F, and G).

Listen to this track which features the band playing the following chord progression.

3.41 Chord Sequence – Chords I, IV, & V

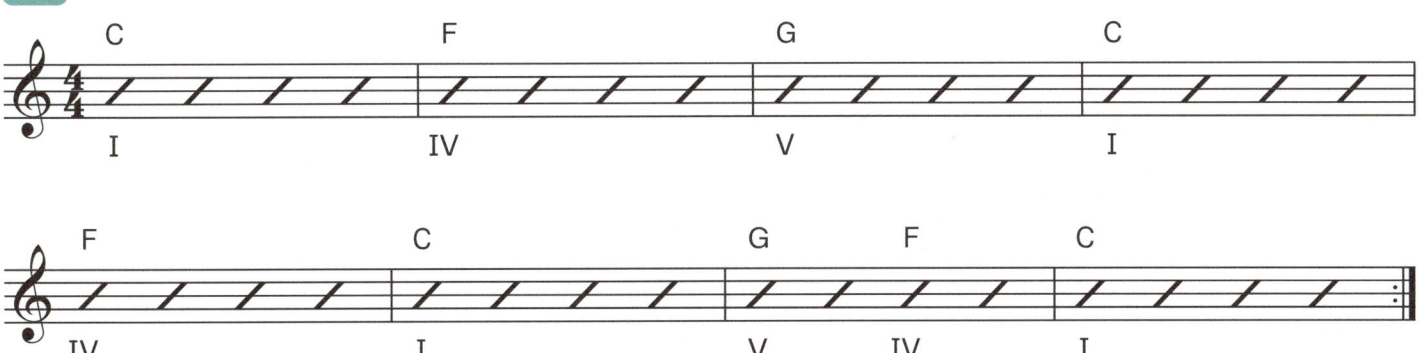

Again, if you are struggling to recognise the chord changes, listen to this track which just contains the bass and drums. Listen specifically to the bass playing the root of each chord.

3.42 Chord Sequence – Chords I, IV, & V (Bass & Drums)

Many songs are constructed using just using chords I, IV, and V – the primary triads. These are primary triads because these three chords combined contain all the notes in the C major scale (C-D-E-F-G-A-B). This means that if the melody was on any note in the major scale, an appropriate chord could be found to harmonise it.

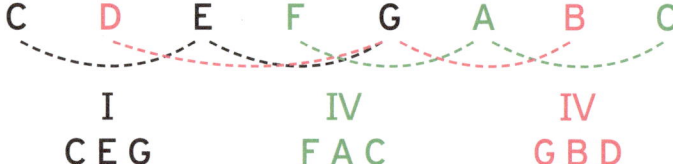

Playlist: Chords I, IV and V

The songs in this Spotify Playlist mainly use chords I, IV, and V.

Note that some of the songs in this playlist are not in the key of C major, however, if the songs were transposed into the key of C, the main chords would be C, F, and G.

- Ritchie Valens: La Bamba
- The Beatles: Twist And Shout
- The Kingsmen: Louie Louie
- Counting Crows: Hanginaround
- U2: I Still Haven't Found What I'm Looking For
- Etta James: Next Door To The Blues

Spotlight

In all the examples so far, the first chord has always been chord I of the key. By no means is this always the case, but it is a good starting point for writing your own progressions.

Exercise: Hear the Changes (Part 3)

Listen to each track which contains a chord progression played by a band. The chord progression includes chords I, IV, and V and all the progressions begin on chord I.

Write in the Roman numerals and the chord symbols. The key signatures and time signatures have been provided for you.

Exercise 1 (4 bars) D major (chords I, IV, and V)

3.43 Hear the Changes (Part 3) Ex. 1

Harmony

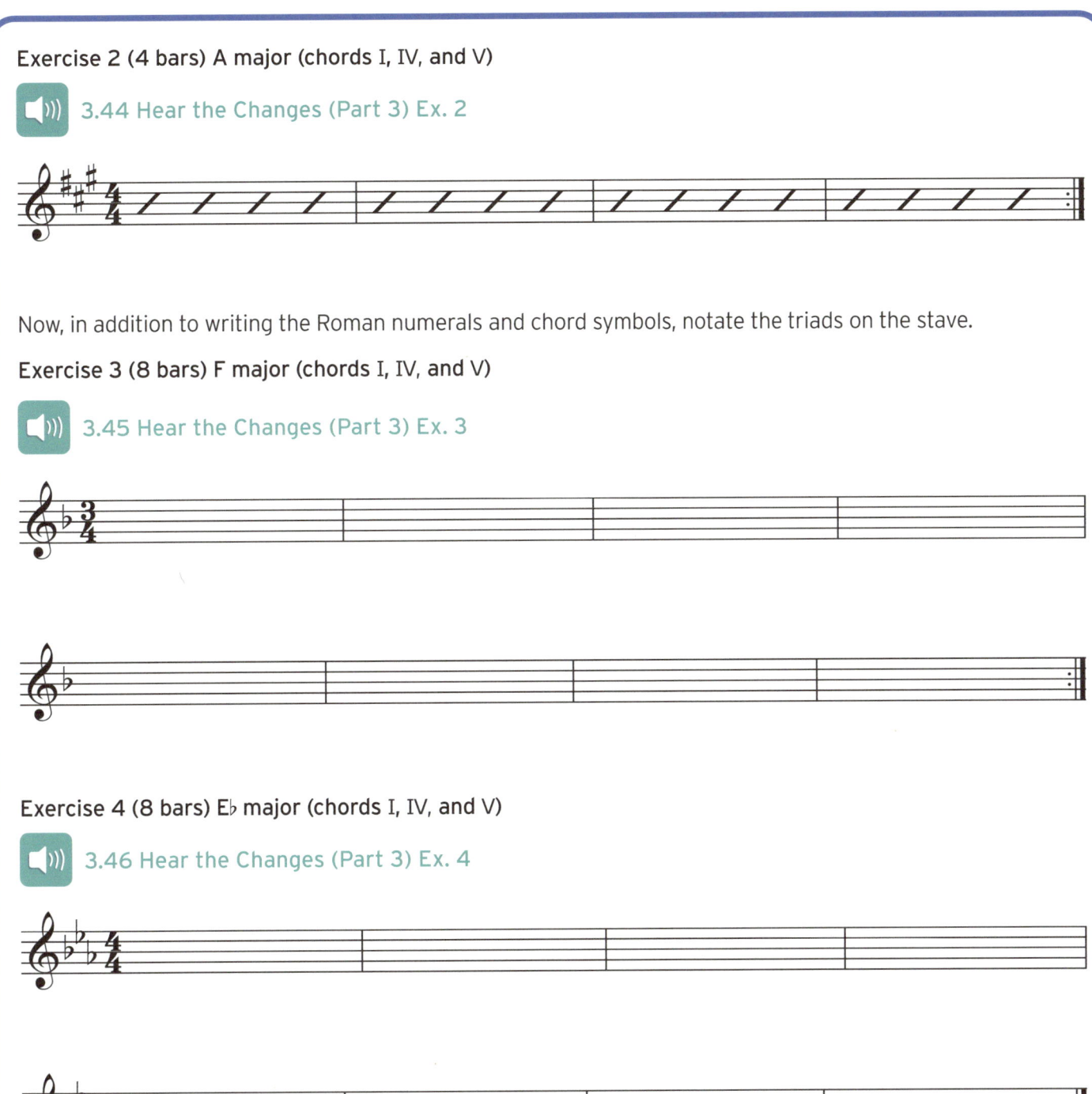

Exercise 2 (4 bars) A major (chords I, IV, and V)

🔊 3.44 Hear the Changes (Part 3) Ex. 2

Now, in addition to writing the Roman numerals and chord symbols, notate the triads on the stave.

Exercise 3 (8 bars) F major (chords I, IV, and V)

🔊 3.45 Hear the Changes (Part 3) Ex. 3

Exercise 4 (8 bars) E♭ major (chords I, IV, and V)

🔊 3.46 Hear the Changes (Part 3) Ex. 4

Answers can be found online, see page 8 for details.

Chord vi (The Relative Minor)

The last harmonic movement we are going to look at is the relative minor. For example, in the key of C, the progression would move between C (tonic) and Am (submediant).

Listen to this track which features the band playing the following chord progression which exclusively uses chords I, IV, V, and vi.

 3.47 Chord Sequence – Chord vi (Relative Minor)

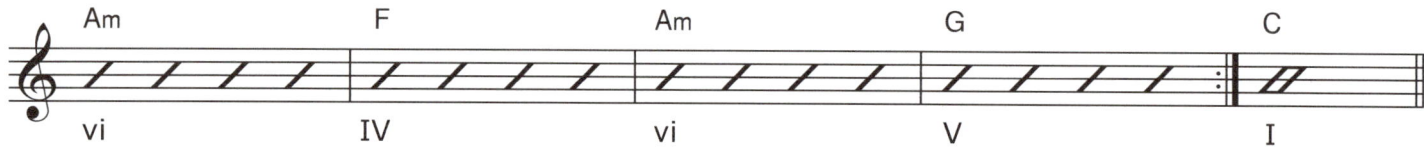

Again, if you are struggling to recognise the chord changes, listen to this track which just contains the bass and drums. Listen specifically to the bass playing the root of each chord.

 3.48 Chord Sequence – Chord vi (Relative Minor) Bass & Drums

Spotlight

Remember that the Roman numerals are lowercase for minor chords – eg, vi.

Let's look at a progression, where chord I is **not** the first chord. Listen to this track which features the band playing the following chord progression which begins on chord vi (the relative minor).

 3.49 Chord Sequence – Beginning on Chord vi

Harmony

Again, if you are struggling to recognise the chord changes, listen to this track which just contains the bass and drums. Listen specifically to the bass playing the root of each chord.

 3.50 Chord Sequence – Beginning on Chord vi (Bass & Drums)

This chord progression is still in the key of C major, even though it begins on A minor. We know this because the progression finishes with a C major chord in the eighth bar.

These chords could be used in any order and still work as a progression.

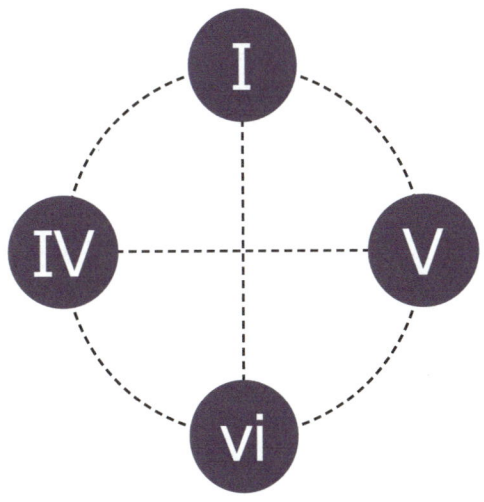

Many songs use these four chords. There are several examples on YouTube of comedy groups putting together a string of songs showing just how common it is to use just these four chords.

 Playlist: Chords I, IV, V, and vi

The songs in this Spotify Playlist mainly use chords I, IV, V, and vi.

Note that some of the songs in this playlist are not in the key of C major, however, if the songs were transposed into the key of C, the main chords would be C, F, G, and Am.

- Bob Marley & The Wailers: No Woman No Cry
- U2: With Or Without You
- John Denver: Take Me Home, Country Roads
- Jason Mraz: I'm Yours
- Taylor Swift: All Too Well
- Lewis Capaldi: Someone You Loved
- Maroon 5: She Will Be Loved
- The Beatles: Let It Be
- Adele: Someone Like You
- Emeli Sandé: Read All About It, Pt. III

Exercise: Hear the Changes (Part 4)

Listen to each track which contains a chord progression played by a band. The chord progression includes chords I, IV, V, and vi.

Write in the Roman numerals and the chord symbols. The key signatures and time signatures have been provided for you, as well as the first chord in each sequence.

Exercise 1 (4 bars) D major (chords I, IV, V, and vi)

 3.51 Hear the Changes (Part 4) Ex. 1

Exercise 2 (4 bars) G major (chords I, IV, V, and vi)

 3.52 Hear the Changes (Part 4) Ex. 2

Exercise 3 (8 bars) B♭ major (chords I, IV, V, and vi)

Now, in addition to writing the Roman numerals and chord symbols, notate the triads on the stave. The chord progression will either start on chord I or chord vi of the key (if the chord progression begins on a major chord, it will be chord I; if the chord progression begins on a minor chord, it will be chord vi).

 3.53 Hear the Changes (Part 4) Ex. 3

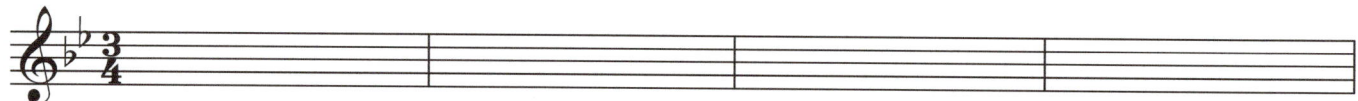

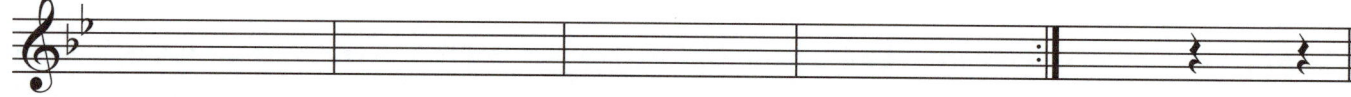

Harmony

Exercise 4 (8 bars) A major (chords I, IV, V, and vi)

 3.54 Hear the Changes (Part 4) Ex. 4

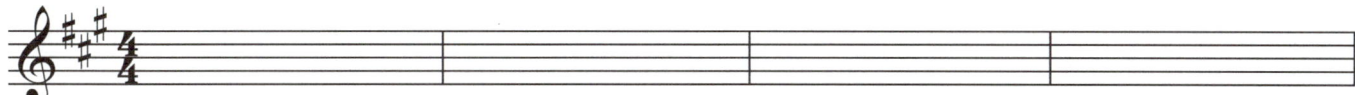

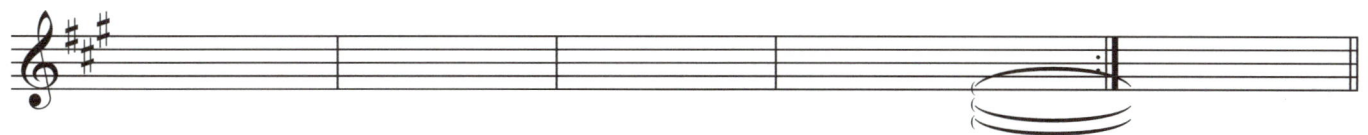

Answers can be found online, see page 8 for details.

? Questions

Here are some questions on the topics covered so far.

1. What is **chord** IV in the key of **E major**?
2. What chord is **E** in the key of **A major**?
3. What is **chord** vi in the key of **B♭ major**?
4. What chord is **E♭** in **A♭ major**?
5. What is **chord** IV in the key of **F major**?
6. What chord is **B♭m** in the key of **D♭ major**?
7. What is **chord** V in the key of **D major**?
8. What chord is **D** in the key of **A major**?
9. What is **chord** vi in the key of **G♭ major**?
10. What chord is **Gm** in the key of **F major**?

Answers can be found online, see page 8 for details.

The 12-Bar Blues

The 12-bar blues or twelve-bar blues, which emerged in the early 20th century among African-American musicians in the Southern states of America, reflects the experiences and emotions of the time, including struggles and hardships. This musical structure provided a way for artists to express their feelings and tell stories about their lives. Over time, it became a fundamental and widely recognised musical structure with a significant influence on various music genres, including rock, pop, and jazz.

The 12-bar blues is designed to repeat, often forming the entire harmonic framework for a song. There are several variations, but arguably the most common version of the sequence is shown below.

Standard 12-Bar Blues

Listen to this track which demonstrates the **standard 12-bar blues** which uses chords I, IV, and V. Here it is in the key of C.

 3.55 12-Bar Blues in C

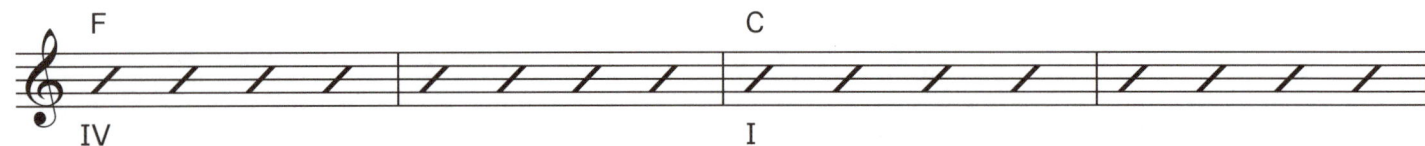
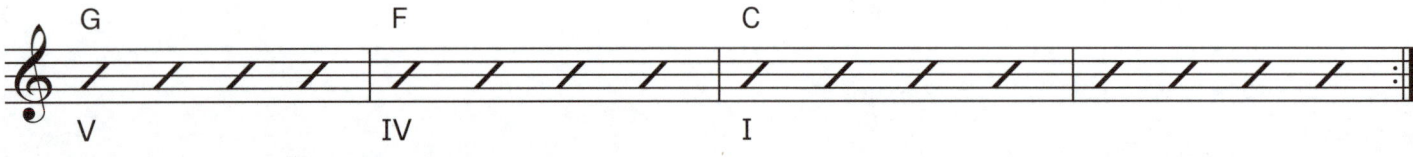

Harmony

Quick-Change Variation

A 'quick change' refers to a variation in the standard 12-bar blues chord progression. Specifically, it means that the IV chord appears in bar 2 for the duration of one bar, before returning back to chord I.

Listen to this track which demonstrates a band playing a 12-bar blues in the key of C with a 'quick change' in bar 2.

 3.56 12-Bar Blues in C with a Quick Change

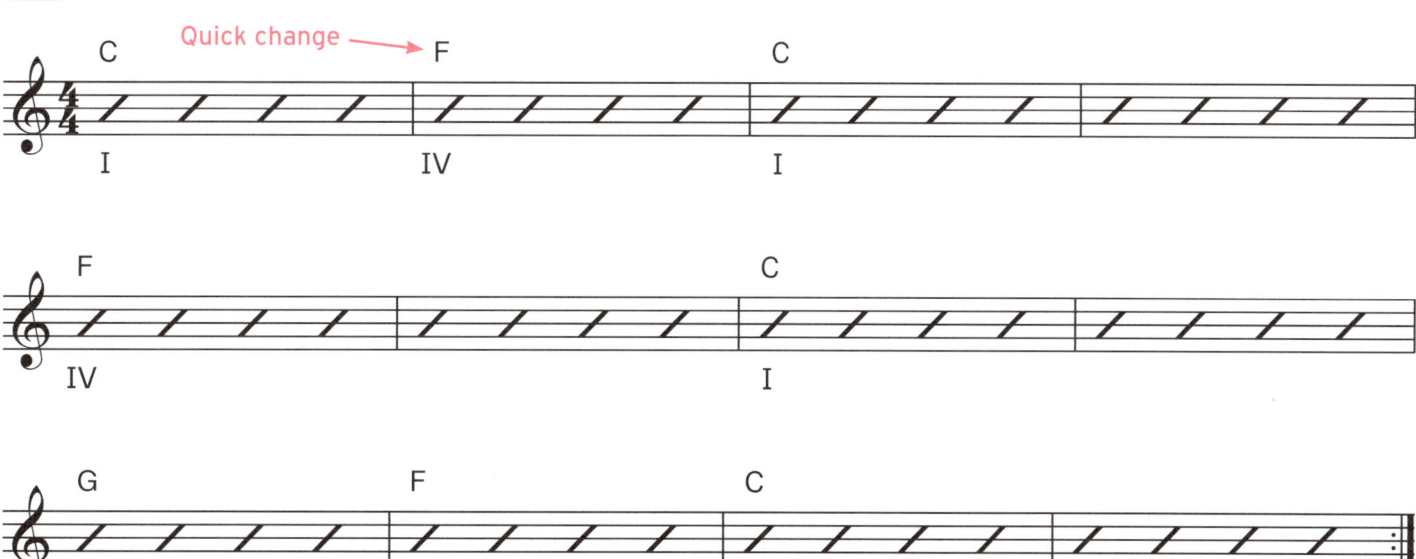

Exercise: Notating Chords of the Blues

Write in the triads under the chord symbols for this 12-bar blues with a quick-change variation. Remember that the chord symbol doesn't need to be restated in each bar if the chord stays the same (eg bar 4 is also a C chord).

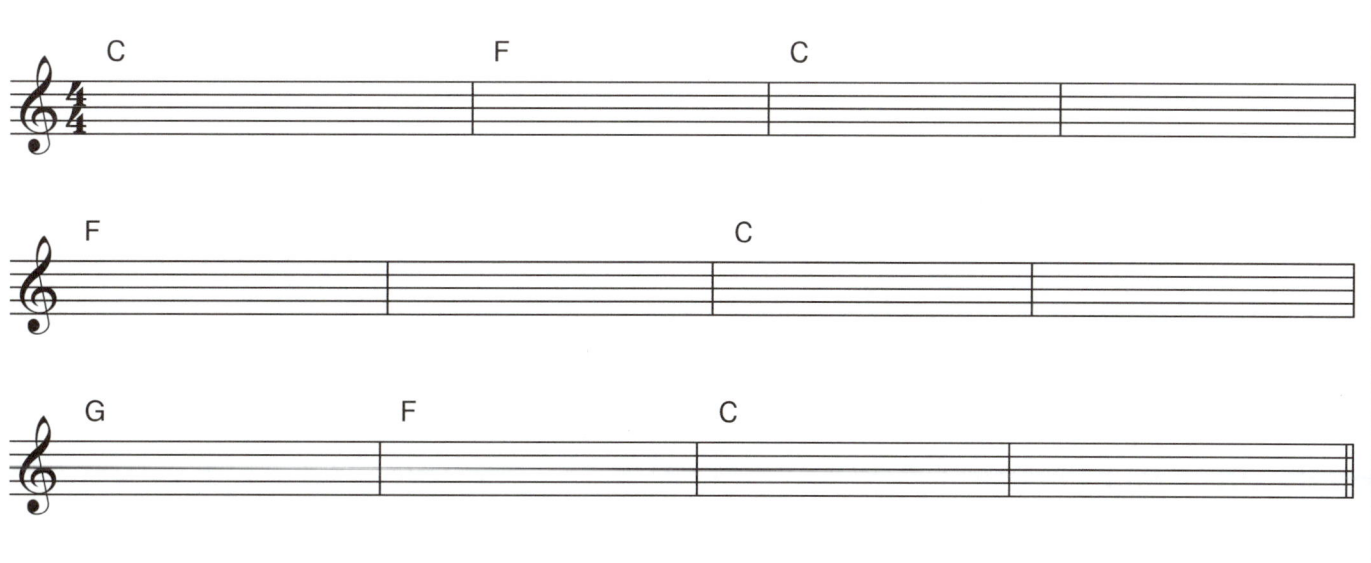

Answers can be found online, see page 8 for details.

Long V Chord Variation

A 'long V' chord refers to a variation in the final four bars of a 12-bar blues. Here, the V chord lasts for two bars and then resolves to chord I.

Listen to this track which demonstrates a band playing a 12-bar blues in the key of C with a 'long V' chord at the end of the sequence.

 3.57 12-Bar Blues in C with a Long V Chord

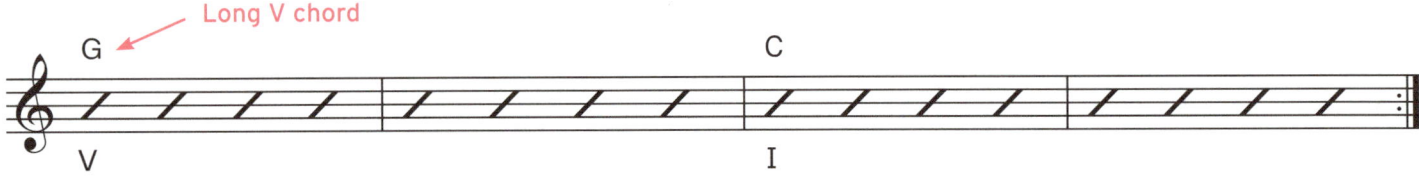

 **Spotlight**

Note in the example above, the sequence also includes a 'quick change' in the second bar.

Harmony

ii-V-I Variation

This variation replaces the V-IV-I in the final four bars of the sequence. Instead a ii–V–I sequence is used, so in the key of C major, this would be **Dm-G-C**.

Listen to this track which demonstrates a band playing a 12-bar blues in the key of C with a ii–V–I progression at the end of the sequence.

 3.58 12-Bar Blues in C with a ii-V-I

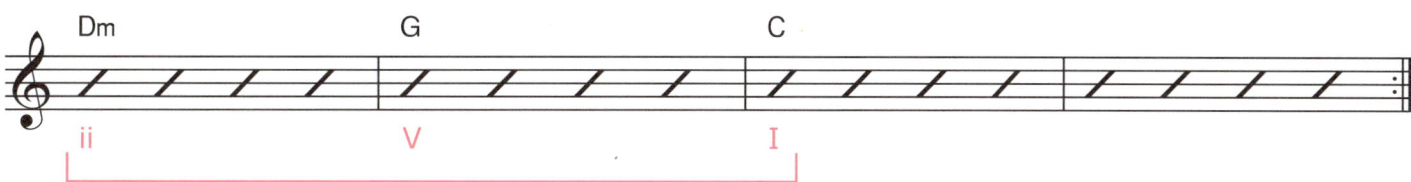

Spotlight

Remember that the Roman numerals are lowercase for minor chords, eg, vi.
Again, note in the example above, the sequence also includes a 'quick change' in the second bar.

Playlist: 12-Bar Blues

The songs in this Spotify Playlist are based around the 12-bar blues.

- Ray Charles: What'd I Say, Pt. 1 & 2
- Prince: Kiss
- Queen: I Want To Break Free
- James Brown & The Famous Flames: I Got You (I Feel Good)
- Big Joe Turner: Shake, Rattle and Roll
- Duffy: Mercy
- Big Mama Thornton: Hound Dog

Exercise: 12-Bar Blues

Write the chord symbols above the stave for the following 12-bar blues sequences.

Exercise 1: Standard 12-bar blues in G major

Exercise 2: 12-bar blues in F major, with a quick-change

Exercise 3: 12-bar blues in D major, with a quick-change and a long V chord

Exercise 4: 12-bar blues in B♭ major, with a quick-change and a ii-V-I

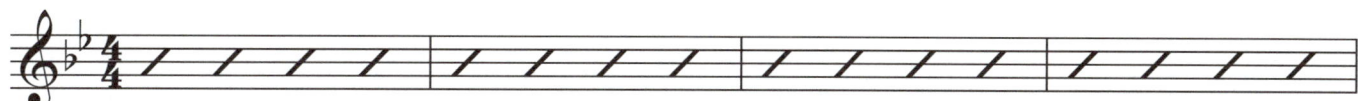

Answers can be found online, see page 8 for details.

Exercise: Transcribe the 12-Bar Blues

Listen to each track which demonstrates a 12-bar blues played by a band. **Write in the chord symbols above the stave.** The key is provided for you. Listen out for the various variations (quick-change, long V chord, and the ii-V-I).

Exercise 1: D major

 3.59 12-Bar Blues in D Ex. 1

Exercise 2: B♭ major

 3.60 12-Bar Blues in B♭ Ex. 2

Harmony

Exercise 3: F major

🔊 3.61 12-Bar Blues in F Ex. 3

Exercise 4: G major

🔊 3.62 12-Bar Blues in G Ex. 4

Answers can be found online, see page 8 for details.

Summary

Being able to recognise chord progressions by ear is a very useful skill. It allows you to play songs without relying on sheet music or chord charts and also helps you understand the structure and harmony of songs, making it easier to perform and adapt to different musical situations.

It is important to be able to recognise chords I, IV, V, and vi within a key as many more complex chord progressions are based around these four chords. Think of them like pillars – it's likely that in most songs these chords will be included, in one form or another.

Experiment with writing your own chord sequences in various keys. Go through the Spotify playlists included in this section and try transcribing the chord sequences, then play along with the tracks. If you incorporate these exercises into your practice regime it will hugely help to develop your ears and your aural awareness.

Melody

The melody is the main musical theme, or tune, in a piece of music. Melodies are made up of a series of notes, and how these notes are arranged in terms of pitch and rhythm gives each melody its unique character.

The melody is often the part of the piece of music that is most recognisable; some tunes are described as being catchy or memorable. A strong melody is sometimes referred to as an 'earworm' – a tune that sticks in our minds and makes us want to sing along after only a few listens.

There is no single 'correct' way to write a melody and songwriters have many different approaches. Some start by humming or singing what sounds good to them, others begin with a chord sequence and then work out notes that fit with the underlying chords.

Melodies often start with the human voice – even instrumental melodies should be able to be sung. Good melodies often feel like they're taking you on a musical journey, almost like telling a story.

In this section, we'll explore how melodies work, and provide you with some strategies to help you generate your own.

Melodic Movement

In simple terms, when moving from one note to the next, a melody can either:

- Go upwards in pitch
- Go downwards in pitch
- Remain on the same pitch (repeat).

Listen to this track which demonstrates a melody in C major, played on guitar. Notice how notes in the melody either remain on the same pitch or move in an upwards or downwards direction.

🔊 4.01 Melody on Guitar

Spotlight

If a melody is in the key of C major, it means it's likely that the majority of the notes are from the C major scale.

In the example on page 139, all the notes in the C major scale are used apart from the 7th degree (B natural). Notice how the melody doesn't necessarily have to start on a C. In this case, the melody starts on a G natural (the 5th of the C major scale).

Extra Info

A motif is a short, recurring musical idea or pattern that adds character and memorability to a melody. It's like a musical building block that gets repeated to create a recognisable tune. For example, in the melody on page 139 the rhythm of the first bar is repeated at several points throughout the eight bars. This helps to strengthen the tune.

When crafting your own melodies, motifs can be a powerful tool for melody development. You can create more engaging melodies by incorporating recurring rhythmic patterns while altering the notes in the melody to add variety and interest.

Steps vs Leaps

When a melody is moving either upwards or downwards in pitch, the melody can move by a step or a leap.

Steps

A step is the smallest interval between two consecutive notes. For example, in the key of C major, a step away from C would be B or D, and a step away from G would be F or A.

Spotlight

Note that this is the smallest step within a diatonic scale (either a semitone or a tone).

Melody

Here is an example of a diatonic melody featuring entirely stepwise movement.

Listen to this track which demonstrates the following melody played on guitar. Each note in the melody is either a repeated note, or the next note in the scale in an upwards or downwards direction. This melody uses the first five notes of the C major scale (C, D, E, F, and G). Here the melody begins and ends on the tonic I.

 4.02 Melody with Stepwise Movement in C

Here is another example of a 4-bar melody, this time in the key of F major. Each note in the melody is either a repeated note, or the next note in the scale in an upwards or downwards direction. This melody uses all the notes in the F major scale (F, G, A, B♭, C, D, and E). Here the melody beings on the 5th of the scale (C) and ends on the tonic (F).

 4.03 Melody with Stepwise Movement in F

Both melodies use a limited range. The range of a melody is the distance between the highest note and the lowest note. The range can affect the overall shape of a melody – for the moment we will aim to keep our melodies within the range of one octave. Melodies that have too broad a range are difficult to sing and therefore sound stretched out and awkward.

Extra Info

Notice how the melodies above use a mixture of note values (crotchets, minims, quavers, and semiquavers). This can help make the melody more rhythmically interesting.

Exercise: Melody Writing (Steps)

Write your own melody using entirely stepwise movement. Start by considering which direction you would like your melody to travel (upwards or downwards). Remember that a melody can also stay on the same note.

Look at the key signature before you begin writing, keep the melody within an octave range, and aim to include different note values to add rhythmic interest. End your melody on the keynote.

A time signature and key signature has been provided for you.

Exercise 1 (4 bars): the first bar of this melody has been provided for you.

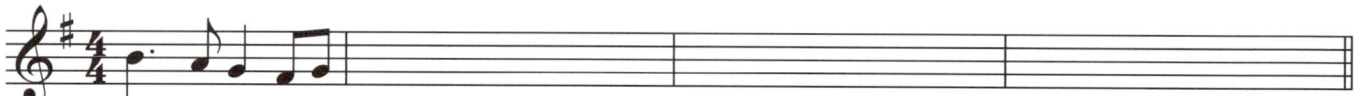

Exercise 2 (4 bars): the first bar of this melody has been provided for you.

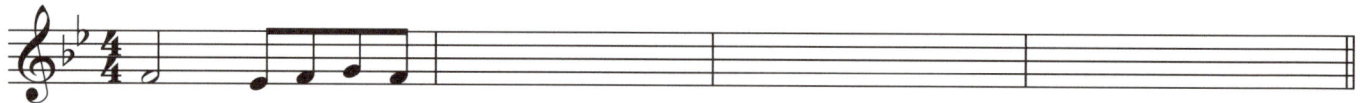

Exercise 3 (4 bars): the first note of this melody has been provided for you.

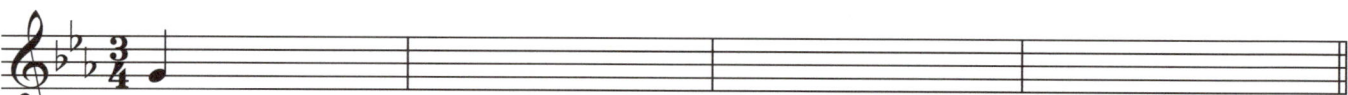

Exercise 4 (8 bars): the first note of this melody has been provided for you.

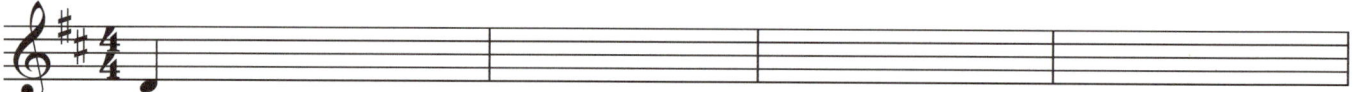

Once you have finished writing your melody, sing or play it back. Are there any sections of the melody that you feel work better than others?

This is a creative exercise, so there are no 'answers'.

Melody

Leaps

A leap is any interval larger than a step. For example, in the key of C major, a leap away from C would be any note, in any direction apart from B or D.

Here is an example of a melody in B♭ major, featuring a number of leaps. Listen to this track which demonstrates the following melody played on guitar.

 4.04 Melody with Leaps in B♭

This melody uses all the notes in the B♭ major scale (B♭, C, D, E♭, F, G, A). Here the melody begins on the 5th of the scale (F) and ends on the tonic (B♭).

 **Extra Info**

The size of the leaps within this melody vary. The first leap (F-D) is a major 6th. The second leap (D-F) is a minor 3rd and the third leap (G-E♭) is a minor 6th.

Notice how the melody also features stepwise movement.

Here is another example of a 4-bar melody, this time in the key of A major. Listen to this track which demonstrates the melody played on guitar.

This melody uses all the notes in the A major scale, apart from the 7th degree (A, B, C♯, D, E, F♯). Here the melody beings on the 3rd of the scale (C♯) and also ends on the 3rd of the scale (C♯).

 4.05 Melody with Leaps in A

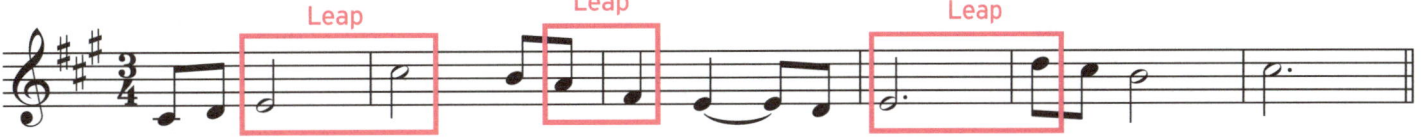

Too many leaps can make a melody sound angular and disjointed.

Extra Info

Again, the size of the leaps within this melody vary. The first leap (E-C♯) is a major 6th. The second leap (A-F♯) is a minor 3rd and the third leap (E-D) is a minor 7th.

This melody also features stepwise movement, however, the range of this melody is slightly larger than an octave. The lowest note is a C♯ and the highest note is a D natural. This interval is one semitone larger than an octave (a minor 9th).

Exercise: Finding Steps and Leaps

Pick one of your favourite songs and try to transcribe 4 bars of the melody. Circle any notes that move by step, and put a box around any leaps.

This is a creative exercise, so there are no 'answers'.

Melody

Exercise: Melody Writing (Leaps)

Write your own melody using a mixture of stepwise movement and leaps. Start by considering which direction you would like your melody to travel (upwards or downwards). Remember that a melody can also stay on the same note.

Look at the key signature before you begin writing, keep the melody within an octave range, and aim to include different note values to add rhythmic interest. A time signature and key signature has been provided for you.

Exercise 1 (4 bars): the first bar of this melody has been provided for you.

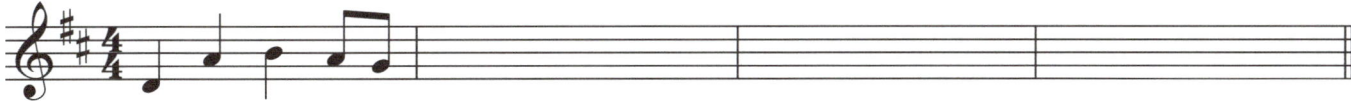

Exercise 2 (4 bars): the first bar of this melody has been provided for you.

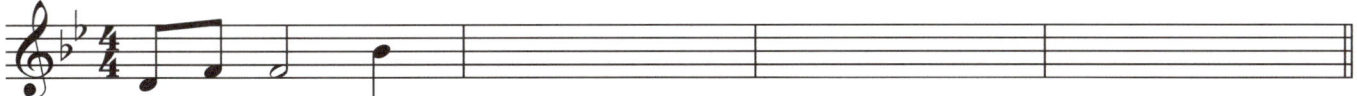

Exercise 3 (4 bars): the first note of this melody has been provided for you.

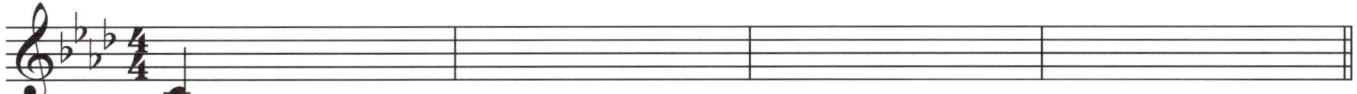

Exercise 4 (8 bars): the first note of this melody has been provided for you.

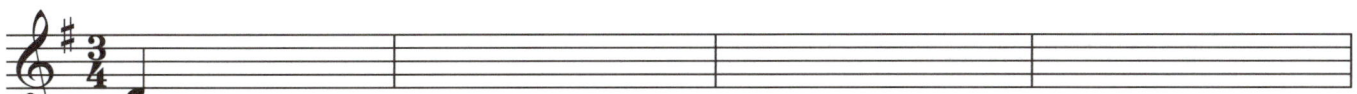

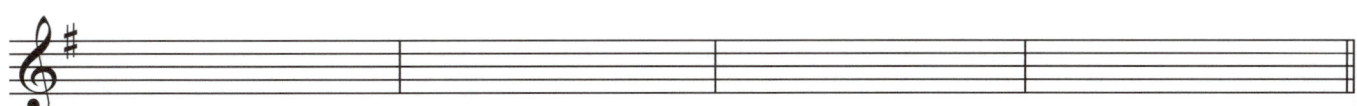

Once you have finished writing your melody, sing or play it back. Are there any sections of the melody that you feel work better than others?

This is a creative exercise, so there are no 'answers'.

Pentatonic Melodies

The pentatonic scale is a simple but powerful tool in music. The scale consists of just **five notes** and is widely used in various music styles. These five notes always sound good together, making the pentatonic scale natural to sing, and a go-to choice for musicians when creating melodies or improvising. The pentatonic scale is a musical pattern that's found in many cultures around the world.

The word 'pentatonic' comes from the Greek word *pente* meaning 'five'. The major pentatonic scale is like the major scale, except the 4th and 7th degrees are removed.

Listen to this track which demonstrates the C major pentatonic scale ascending and descending.

 4.06 C Major Pentatonic Scale

C Major Pentatonic

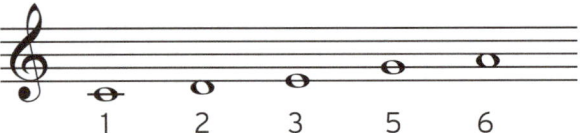

Extra Info

The major scale contains two semitone intervals between the 3rd and 4th, and the 7th and 8th degrees. Semitone intervals are sometimes thought of as dissonant intervals. When you play the notes of a semitone together, they don't sound as stable as say a 3rd, or a 5th.

In the pentatonic scale these dissonant, semitone intervals have been removed. This creates a simple scale that is smooth and easy to layer over different chords.

Search on YouTube for 'Bobby McFerrin Pentatonic' to see how people have a natural and instinctive understanding of the pentatonic scale.

Playlist: Major Pentatonic Melodies

The following playlist features songs that have major pentatonic melodies.

- Stevie Wonder: Sir Duke (does contain some chromaticism)
- Jack Johnson: Better Together
- The Temptations: My Girl
- LeAnn Rimes: Amazing Grace

Melody

Here is an example of a melody that uses the B♭ pentatonic scale. The melody begins and ends on the tonic (B♭) and the range of the melody is one octave.

Listen to this track which demonstrates the melody played on guitar.

 4.07 B♭ Pentatonic Melody

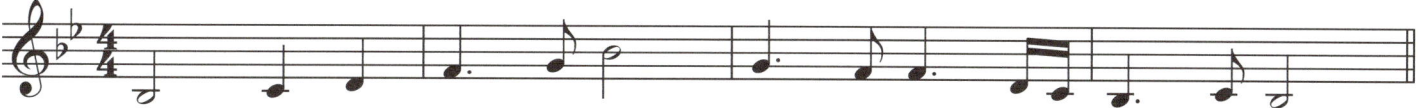

Here is an example of a melody that uses the F pentatonic scale. The melody begins and ends on the 3rd (A) and the range of the melody is one octave.

Listen to this track which demonstrates the melody played on piano.

 4.08 F Pentatonic Melody

Here is another melody that uses the pentatonic scale, this time in the key of G major. The melody begins and ends on the 5th (D).

Listen to this track which demonstrates the melody played on guitar.

 4.09 G Pentatonic Melody

 **Extra Info**

While melodies can begin on any note within the key, a good starting point is to begin on the tonic, 3rd, or 5th of the key as these notes establish a strong a sense of 'home' for the listener and will provide a strong foundation for your tune.

Transcribing melodies, much like transcribing chords, is a valuable skill. It involves the ability to listen to a song and accurately notate the melody, which establishes a vital connection between the sounds you hear and the symbols that represent those sounds on a musical score.

Being able to transcribe a melody means you can document your musical ideas effectively, as without this ability it can become challenging to preserve musical inspirations and ideas that often arrive spontaneously. It's also a great way to communicate your ideas to others!

Exercise: Transcribing Pentatonic Melodies

Listen to each track and transcribe the pentatonic melodies. Each melody will be played through twice.

Before you begin, look at the key signature and work out the notes in the relevant major pentatonic scale. Consider transcribing the rhythm of the melody before you add the pitches.

Exercise 1 (4 bars): the first and third bars of this melody have been provided for you.
The melody only contains crotchet notes or rests.

4.10 Transcribing Pentatonic Melodies Ex. 1

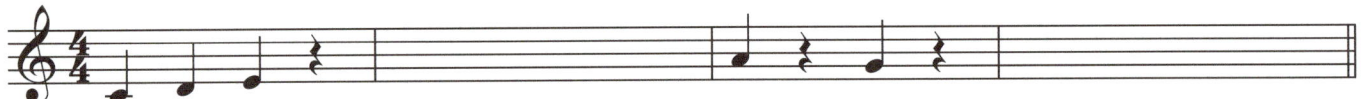

Exercise 2 (4 bars): the first and third bars of this melody have been provided for you.
The melody only contains crotchet notes or rests.

4.11 Transcribing Pentatonic Melodies Ex. 2

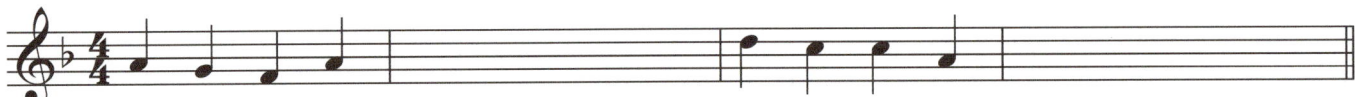

Exercise 3 (4 bars): the first and last bars of this melody have been provided for you.
The missing melody only contains crotchet notes or rests.

4.12 Transcribing Pentatonic Melodies Ex. 3

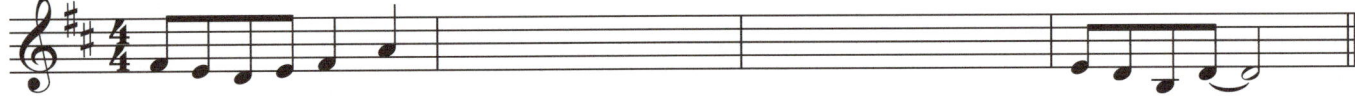

Melody

Exercise 4 (4 bars): the first and last bars of this melody have been provided for you.
The melody only contains crotchet and quaver notes or rests.

 4.13 Transcribing Pentatonic Melodies Ex. 4

Exercise 5 (4 bars): the first note of this melody has been provided for you.
The melody only contains crotchet and quaver notes or rests.

 4.14 Transcribing Pentatonic Melodies Ex. 5

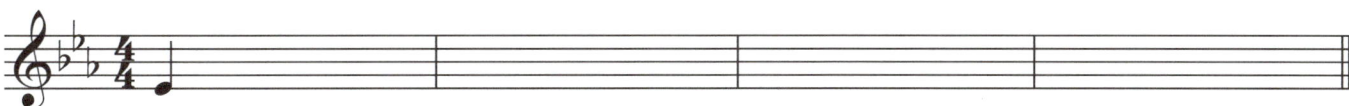

Exercise 6 (4 bars): the first note of this melody has been provided for you.
The melody only contains crotchet and quaver notes or rests.

 4.15 Transcribing Pentatonic Melodies Ex. 6

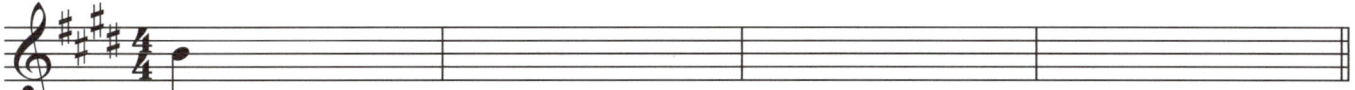

Answers can be found online, see page 8 for details.

Call and Response Melodies

Call and response is a common technique in melody writing that is a kind of conversation between different musical phrases. It's like a musical back-and-forth – or question and answer. In a call and response, one part of the melody, the 'call', plays a musical idea or phrase. Then, another part, known as the 'response', answers back with a different musical idea that complements or contrasts with the call.

Listen to this track which demonstrates a call and response melody over a 12-bar blues in the key of C. Notice how the 'call' leaves the melody hanging, and the 'response' feels like each phrase has concluded.

 4.16 Call and Response Melody on 12-Bar Blues

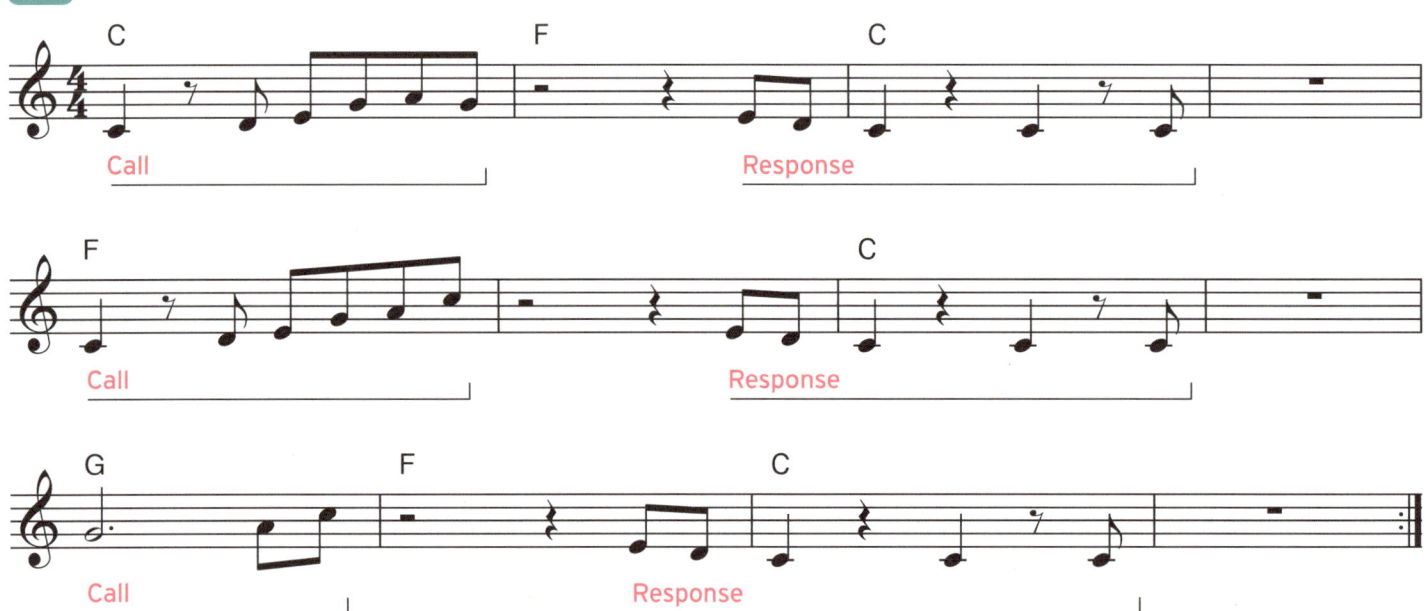

In the above example, the answer phrase is the same each time. This is called repetition. When you repeat parts of a melody, it helps give the melody structure and makes it feel like it all fits together.

If you want to draw attention to a specific part of the music, you can repeat it. This is often done in songs to make certain lines or musical ideas more important.

Melody

Exercise: Call and Response Melodies

Write a melody that uses 'call and response' over the following 12-bar blues sequences.

Before you begin, look at the key signature and work out the notes in the relevant major pentatonic scale. Once you have written your melody, sing or play it with the accompanying track and see how it fits.

The call/response could be the same each time, or you could vary them slightly – it's up to you!

Exercise 1

Write a call (in G major). The answer phrase has been provided for you and is played by the band.

 4.17 Call and Response Melodies Ex. 1

Exercise 2
Write an answer to the following calls in B♭ major. The call has been provided and is played by the band.

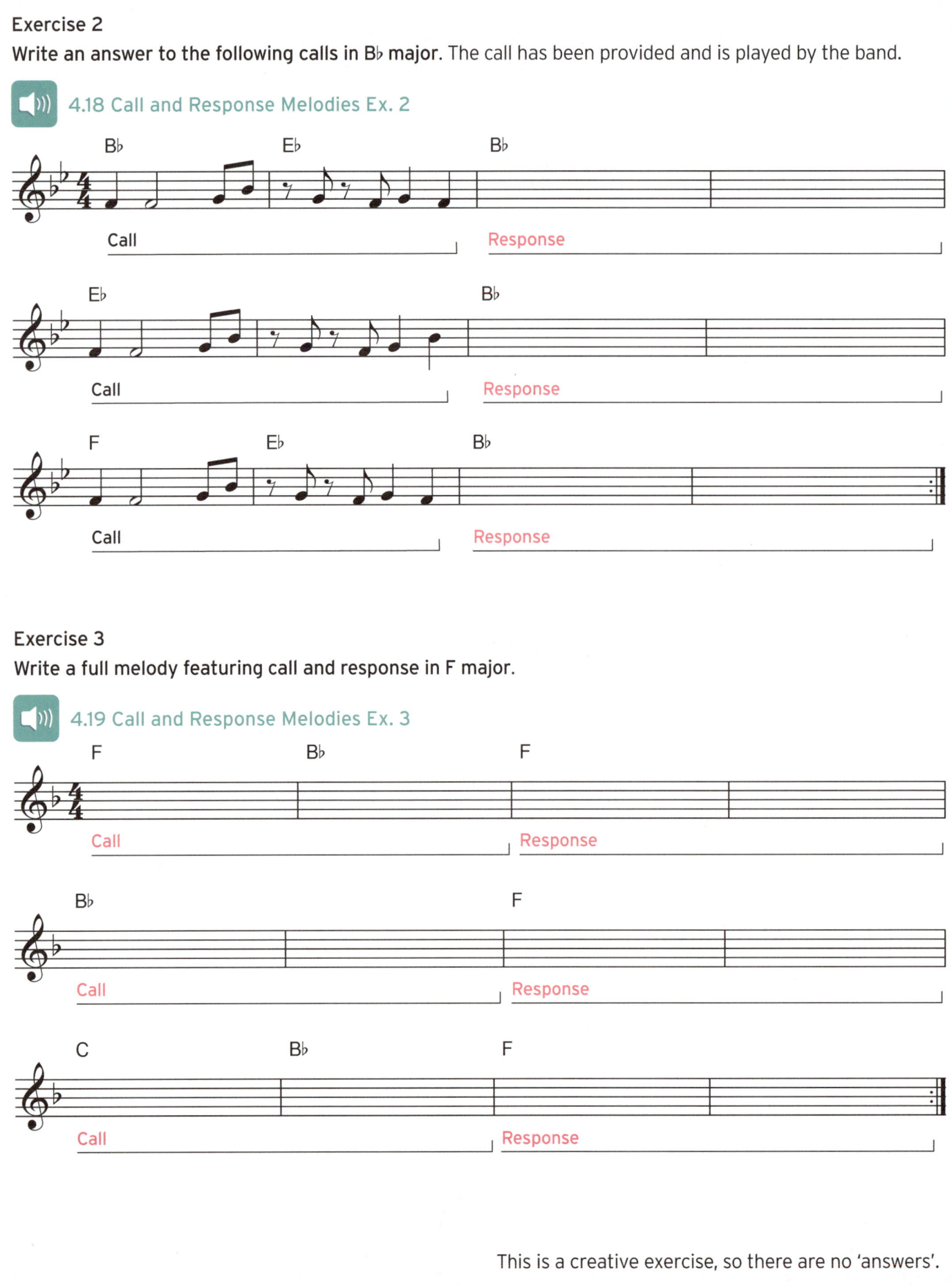

🔊 4.18 Call and Response Melodies Ex. 2

Exercise 3
Write a full melody featuring call and response in F major.

🔊 4.19 Call and Response Melodies Ex. 3

This is a creative exercise, so there are no 'answers'.

Playlist: Call and Response Melodies

The following playlist features songs that incorporate 'call and response' melodies.

- Chuck Berry: School Day (Ring Ring Goes The Bell)
- The Isley Brothers: Shout, Pts. 1 & 2
- The Who: My Generation
- Backstreet Boys: I Want It That Way
- The Mamas & The Papas: California Dreamin'
- Gladys Knight & The Pips: Midnight Train To Georgia

Exercise: Call and Response in Lyrics

Pick one of the songs from the playlist above. Find the lyrics and write out the words to one of the choruses. Put a circle around the 'calls' and a box around the 'responses'.

_____

_____

_____

_____

_____

_____

_____

_____

This is a creative exercise, so there are no 'answers'.

Conclusion

Over the course of this book, we have covered a lot of ground! We began with understanding rhythm and pulse and worked our way up through scales, keys, intervals, and the circle of fifths, to arrive at a point where we can write, transcribe, and notate chord sequences and melodies in a major key.

Do continue to refer to the concepts in this book. I'd recommend going through each of the sections several times to ensure you have a thorough grasp of the concepts.

The second book in this series will focus on more advanced topics. Now we understand the fundamental building blocks, we can move on to looking at more advanced rhythmic, melodic, and harmonic concepts... See you in the next book!

Appendix

Keyboard Diagram

Major Scales – Treble Clef

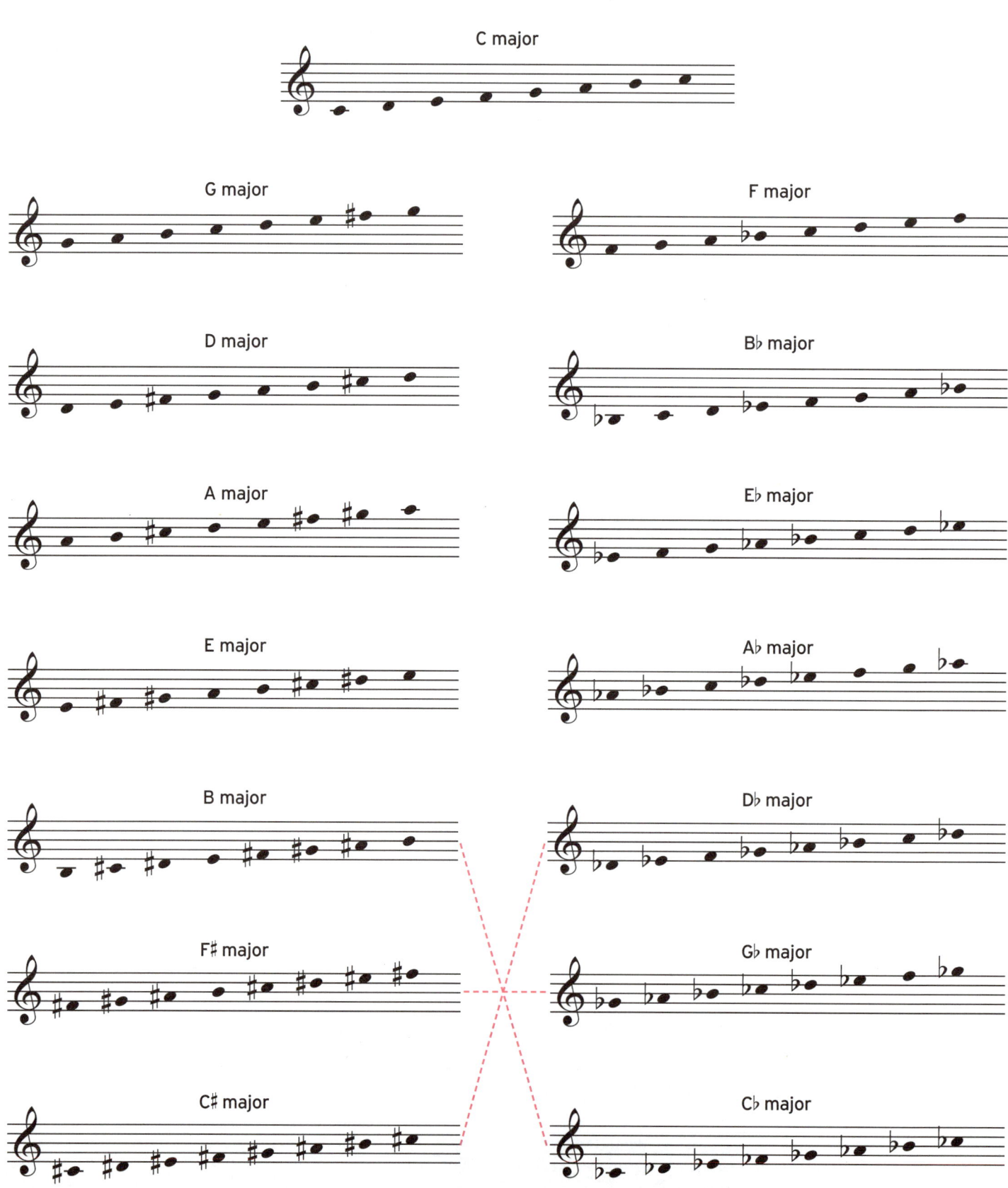

The dashed lines indicate enharmonic equivalents.

Major Scales – Bass Clef

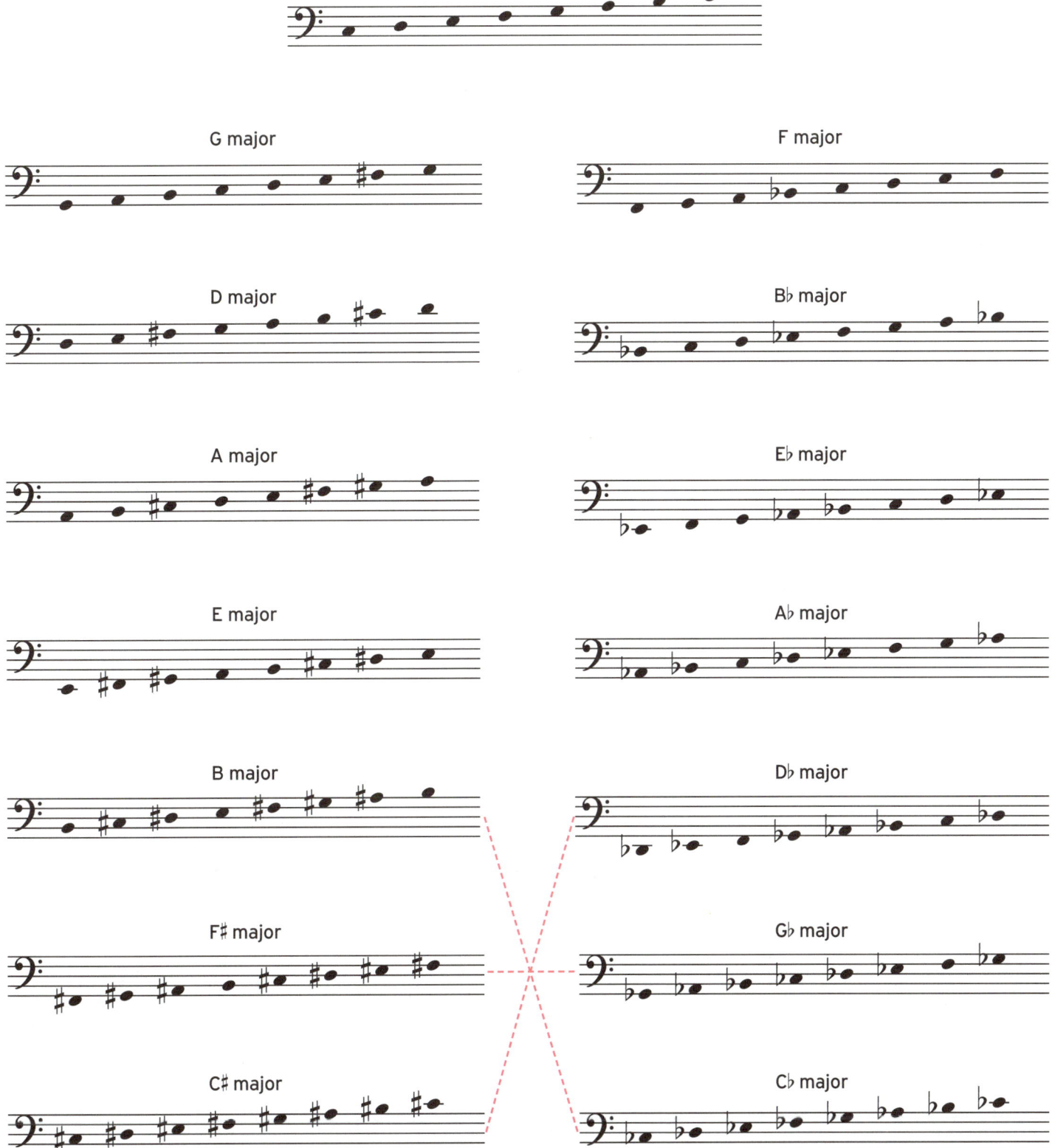

The dashed lines indicate enharmonic equivalents.

Natural Minor Scales – Treble Clef

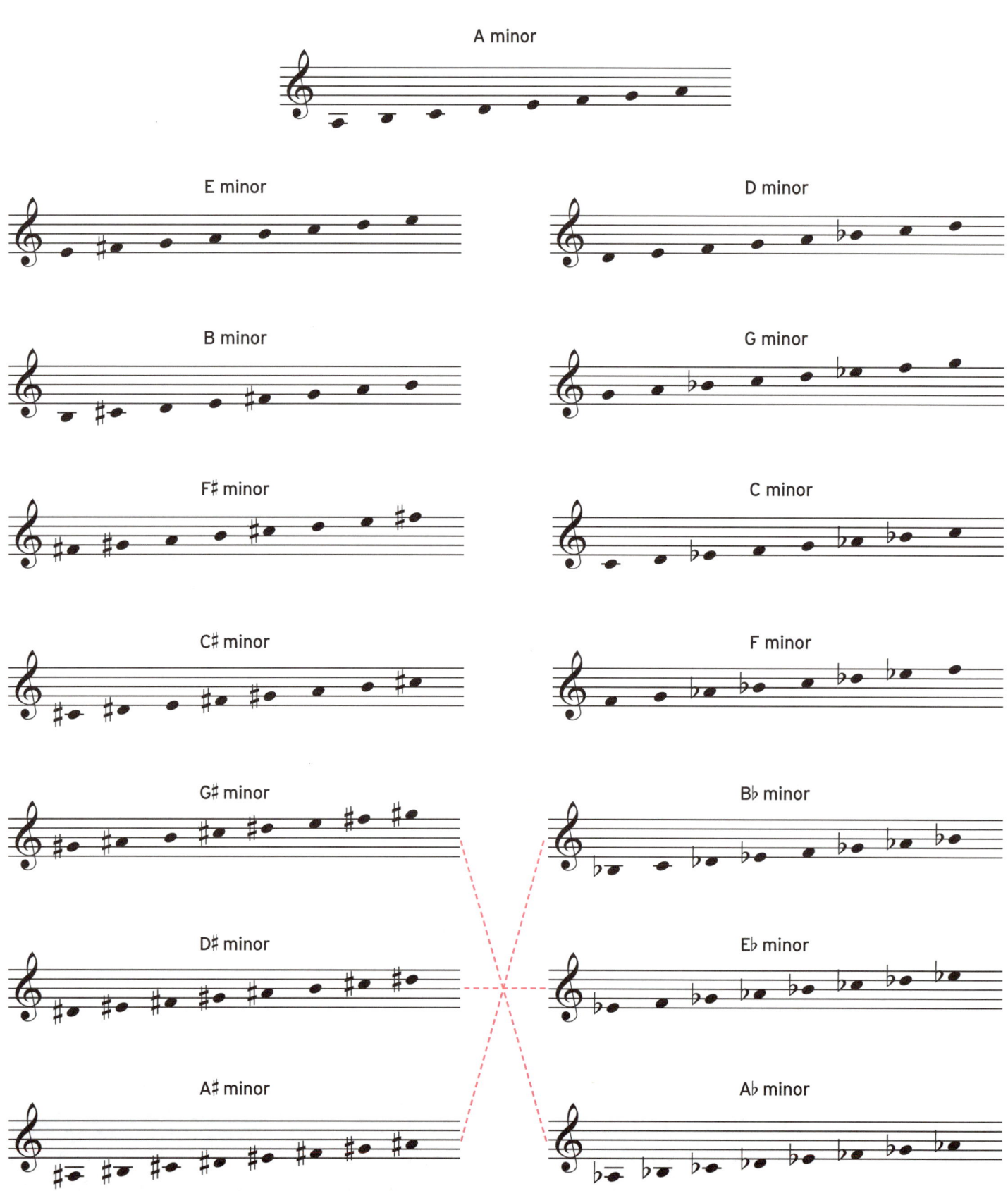

The dashed lines indicate enharmonic equivalents.

Appendix

Natural Minor Scales – Bass Clef

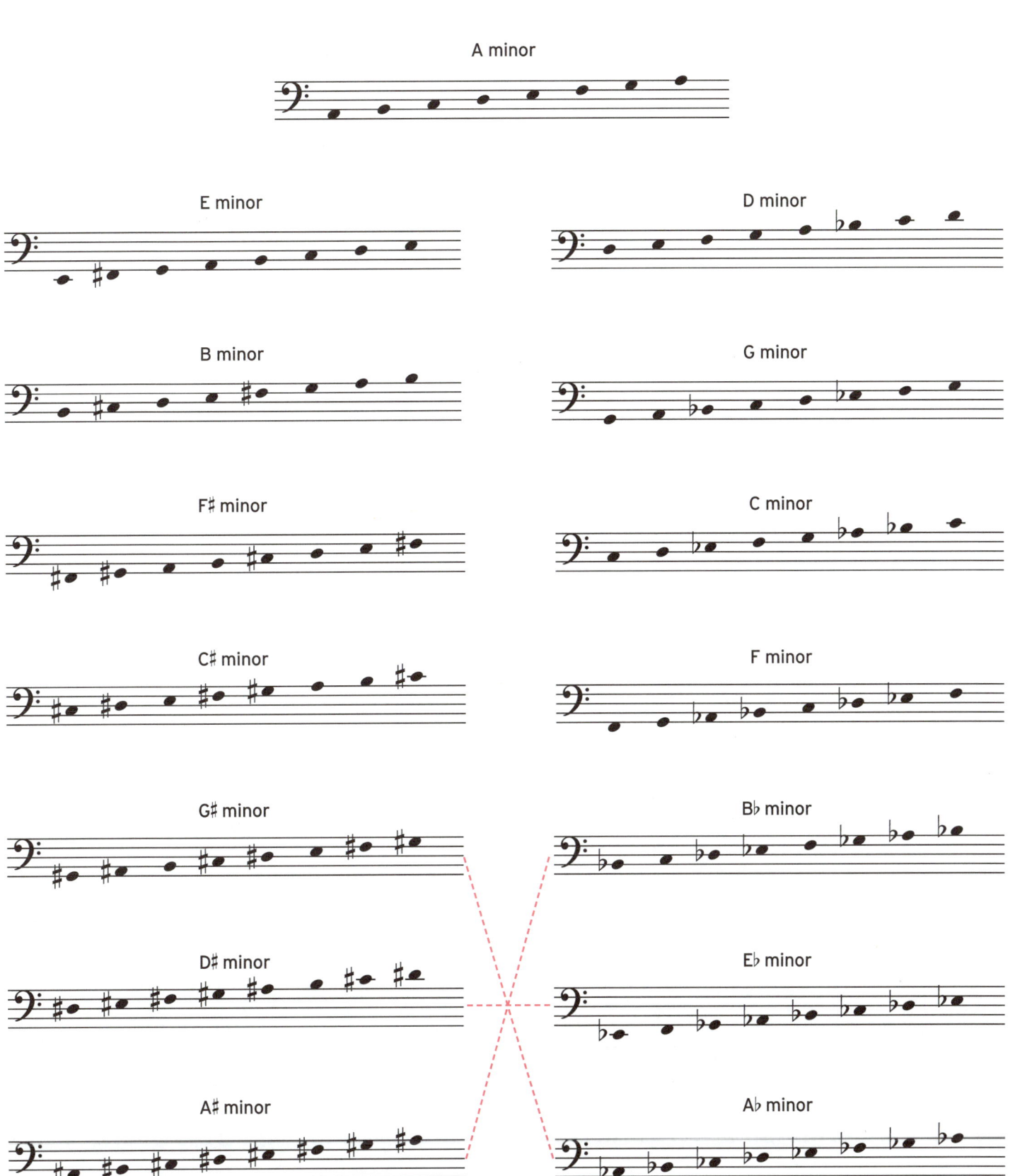

The dashed lines indicate enharmonic equivalents.

Manuscript Paper

Appendix

Glossary

Augmented	A type of interval which is major or perfect and the upper note has been raised by a semitone or half step.
Beam	♫ The line(s) used to connect notes with a duration of a quaver or smaller.
Beaming	The process of connecting notes with a duration of a quaver or smaller.
Changes	An alternative term for 'chord sequence', or 'chord progression'. Often used colloquially.
Chromatic	A scale or part of a scale ascending or descending by semitones; both black and white keys on a piano.
Circle of fifths	A visual tool for organising the 12 chromatic pitches, as a sequence of perfect 5ths.
Count-in	A verbal or instrumental cue used to help the musician(s) establish the initial tempo and time signature of the song. Also known as 'count-off'.
Crotchet	♩ A note held for one beat (British English). Also known as 'quarter note' (American English).
Diatonic	A term used to mean 'of the scale', or 'within the key'.
Diminished	A type of interval which is minor or perfect and the upper note has been lowered by a semitone or half step.
Dominant	The 5th degree of a major or minor scale. Also used to describe chord V.
Eighth-note	♪ A note held for half a beat (American English). Also known as 'quaver' (British English).
Half Note	♩ A note held for two pulse beats (American English). Also known as 'minim' (British English)
Half step	The smallest interval between two notes in Western tonal music (American English). Also known as 'semitone' (British English).
Harmonic interval	An interval where both notes sound at the same time.
Harmony	The sound of two or more notes heard simultaneously.
Imperfect cadence	A chord progression which ends on a dominant chord. Also known as a 'half cadence' (American English).
Interval	The difference in pitch between two sounds.
Keynote	The 1st degree of any diatonic major or minor scale.
Leading note	The 7th degree of a major or minor scale.
Major interval	An interval where the notes are part of the major scale – only 2nds, 3rds, 6ths, and 7ths can be major intervals.

Mediant	The 3rd degree of a major or minor scale.
Melodic interval	An interval where two notes sound one after the other.
Minim	♩ A note held for two pulse beats (British English). Also known as 'half note' (American English).
Minor interval	An interval that is one semitone or half step smaller than a major interval.
Note	In musical notation, a note indicates the pitch and duration of a sound.
Note value	The length or duration of a note.
Notehead	Part of a note – usually circular, indicating pitch and note value.
Octave	An interval between two notes, where the pitch of one note is exactly eight notes higher or lower the pitch of the other.
Perfect cadence	A chord progression where the dominant is followed by the tonic. Also known as an 'authentic cadence' (American English).
Perfect interval	The quality of an interval – only unison, 4th, 5th, and octave intervals can be perfect.
Pitch	A term for how high or low a note sounds.
Plagal cadence	A chord progression where the subdominant is followed by the tonic.
Primary triads	Triads built on the 1st, 4th, or 5th degrees of the scale.
Quarter note	♩ A note held for one beat (American English). Also known as 'crotchet' (British English).
Quaver	♪ A note held for half a beat (British English). Also known as an 'eighth note' (American English).
Root note	The note a chord is constructed from, represented by a capital letter in the chord symbol.
Semibreve	o A note held for four pulse beats (British English). Also known as a 'whole note' (American English).
Semiquaver	♬ A note held for a quarter of a beat (British English). Also known as a '16th-note' (American English).
Semitone	The smallest interval between two notes in Western tonal music (British English). Also known as a 'half step' (American English).
Shuffle	A rhythmic feel, usually in $\frac{12}{8}$
16th note	♬ A note held for a quarter of a beat (American English). Also known as a 'semiquaver' (British English).
Stem	Thin vertical lines, connected to a notehead.
Subdivide	Dividing a rhythmic value into smaller units.

Subdominant	The 4th degree of a major or minor scale.
Submediant	The 6th degree of a major or minor scale.
Supertonic	The 2nd degree of a major or minor scale.
Sus	Short for suspended. The 3rd in a triad is replaced by either the 2nd (sus2) or the 4th (sus4).
Tail	Attached to the stem of the note to indicate whether the note is a quaver (one tail), semiquaver (two tails) or smaller. Also known as a 'flag' (American English).
Tie	A curved line connecting noteheads of the same pitch to extend the duration.
Tone	An interval of two semitones (British English). Also known as a 'whole step' (American English).
Tonic	The 1st degree of a major or minor scale.
Transcribing	The process of listening in-depth to an element of a piece of music, working out how to play it by ear, and then possibly writing it down using a form of notation.
Transpose	The process of moving a collection of notes (eg, a melody and/or chords) to a different key.
Triad	A set of three notes, that when stacked produce a chord.
Tritone	An interval of three tones or whole steps.
Whole note	A note held for four pulse beats (American English). Also known as a 'semibreve' (British English).
Whole step	An interval of two semitones (American English). Also known as a 'tone' (British English).

Recording Credits and Track Listing

Band tracks recorded at Crown Lane Studios, London.

Adam Saunders: Keys; Tommy Emmerton: Guitars; Conor Chaplin: Bass; James Maddren: Drums; John Merriman and Chris Cruz: Engineers.

All other tracks recorded by Simeon Smith.

1.01 Drum Groove
1.02 Drum Groove with Counting
1.03 What's the BPM?
1.04 What's the BPM?
1.05 What's the BPM?
1.06 Crotchet, Quaver, and Semiquaver Note Values
1.07 Crotchet, Quaver, and Semiquaver Rhythm
1.08 Crotchet, Quaver, and Semiquaver Rhythm with Counting
1.09 Read the Rhythm (Part 1) Exercise 1
1.10 Read the Rhythm (Part 1) Exercise 2
1.11 Read the Rhythm (Part 1) Exercise 3
1.12 Read the Rhythm (Part 2) Exercise 1
1.13 Read the Rhythm (Part 2) Exercise 2
1.14 Read the Rhythm (Part 2) Exercise 3
1.15 Rhythm (All Note Values So Far)
1.16 Rhythm (All Note Values So Far) with Counting
1.17 Read the Rhythm (Part 3) Exercise 1
1.18 Read the Rhythm (Part 3) Exercise 2
1.19 Read the Rhythm (Part 3) Exercise 3
1.20 Read the Rhythm (Part 3) Exercise 4
1.21 Transcribe the Rhythm Exercise 1
1.22 Transcribe the Rhythm Exercise 2
1.23 Transcribe the Rhythm Exercise 3
1.24 Transcribe the Rhythm Exercise 4
1.25 Transcribe the Rhythm Exercise 5
1.26 Transcribe the Rhythm Exercise 6
1.27 Transcribe the Rhythm Exercise 7
1.28 Transcribe the Rhythm Exercise 8
1.29 4-Bar Rhythm (Crotchet and Quaver Notes and Rests)
1.30 4-Bar Rhythm (Crotchet and Quaver Notes and Rests) with Counting
1.31 Read the Rhythm (Part 4) Exercise 1
1.32 Read the Rhythm (Part 4) Exercise 2
1.33 Read the Rhythm (Part 4) Exercise 3
1.34 4-Bar Rhythm (Semibreve and Minim Rests)
1.35 4-Bar Rhythm (Semibreve and Minim Rests) with Counting
1.36 4-Bar Rhythm (Crotchets and Semiquaver Rests)
1.37 4-Bar Rhythm (Crotchets and Semiquaver Rests) with Counting
1.38 4-Bar Rhythm (2nd Semiquaver Rests)
1.39 4-Bar Rhythm (2nd Semiquaver Rests) with Counting
1.40 4-Bar Rhythm (3rd Semiquaver Rests)
1.41 4-Bar Rhythm (3rd Semiquaver Rests) with Counting
1.42 4-Bar Rhythm (4th Semiquaver Rests)
1.43 4-Bar Rhythm (4th Semiquaver Rests) with Counting
1.44 4-Bar Rhythm (Every Division Semiquaver Rests)
1.45 4-Bar Rhythm (Every Division Semiquaver Rests) with Counting
1.46 Read the Rhythm (Part 5) Exercise 1
1.47 Read the Rhythm (Part 5) Exercise 2
1.48 Read the Rhythm (Part 5) Exercise 3
1.49 Read the Rhythm (Part 5) Exercise 4
1.50 4-Bar Rhythm (Dotted Minims and Crotchets)
1.51 4-Bar Rhythm (Dotted Minims and Crotchets) with Counting
1.52 Read the Rhythm (Part 6) Exercise 1
1.53 Read the Rhythm (Part 6) Exercise 2
1.54 Read the Rhythm (Part 6) Exercise 3
1.55 Read the Rhythm (Part 6) Exercise 4
1.56 4-Bar Rhythm (Dotted Notes)
1.57 4-Bar Rhythm (Dotted Notes) with Counting
1.58 Read the Rhythm (Part 7) Exercise 1
1.59 Read the Rhythm (Part 7) Exercise 2
1.60 Read the Rhythm (Part 7) Exercise 3
1.61 Read the Rhythm (Part 7) Exercise 4
1.62 Read the Rhythm (Part 8) Exercise 1
1.63 Read the Rhythm (Part 8) Exercise 2
1.64 Read the Rhythm (Part 8) Exercise 3
1.65 Read the Rhythm (Part 8) Exercise 4
1.66 What's the Time Signature? Exercise 1
1.67 What's the Time Signature? Exercise 2
1.68 What's the Time Signature? Exercise 3
2.01 Drum Groove at 105 BPM
2.02 Chromatic Scale on Piano
2.03 Semitones on Piano
2.04 Semitones on Guitar & Bass Guitar
2.05 Tones on Piano
2.06 Tones on Guitar & Bass Guitar
2.07 C Major Scale on Piano, Guitar & Bass Guitar
2.08 Intervals from C Played Harmonically and Melodically
2.09 Intervals from Eb Played Harmonically and Melodically
2.10 What's the Size of the Interval? (Part 2) Exercise 1
2.11 What's the Size of the Interval? (Part 2) Exercise 2
2.12 What's the Size of the Interval? (Part 2) Exercise 3
2.13 What's the Size of the Interval? (Part 2) Exercise 4
2.14 What's the Size of the Interval? (Part 2) Exercise 5

Appendix

2.15 What's the Size of the Interval? (Part 3) Exercise 1
2.16 What's the Size of the Interval? (Part 3) Exercise 2
2.17 What's the Size of the Interval? (Part 3) Exercise 3
2.18 What's the Size of the Interval? (Part 3) Exercise 4
2.19 What's the Size of the Interval? (Part 3) Exercise 5
2.20 Intervals from C Played Harmonically and Melodically
2.21 Intervals from E Played Harmonically and Melodically
2.22 Intervals (Perfect or Major?)
2.23 Major 3rd Followed by a Minor 3rd
2.24 Major 3rd Followed by an Augmented 3rd
2.25 Minor, Major, and Augmented 2nds
2.26 Minor, Major, and Augmented 3rds
2.27 Minor, Major, and Augmented 6ths
2.28 Minor, Major, and Augmented 7ths
2.29 Intervals (Minor, Major or Augmented?)
2.30 Perfect 5th Followed by a Diminished 5th
2.31 Perfect 5th Followed by an Augmented 5th
2.32 Diminished, Perfect, and Augmented Unisons
2.33 Diminished, Perfect, and Augmented 4ths
2.34 Diminished, Perfect, and Augmented 5ths
2.35 Diminished, Perfect, and Augmented 8ves
2.36 Intervals (Diminished, Perfect or Augmented?)
2.37 Circle of Fifths Progression
2.38 C Major Scale (Piano & Guitar)
2.39 A Natural Minor Scale (Piano & Guitar)
2.40 G Natural Minor Scale
3.01 G Major Triad
3.02 Bb Major Triad
3.03 Major Triads Exercise 1
3.04 Major Triads Exercise 2
3.05 G Minor Triad
3.06 Bb Minor Triad
3.07 Minor Triads Exercise 1
3.08 Minor Triads Exercise 2
3.09 Major or Minor Triad? Exercise 1
3.10 Major or Minor Triad? Exercise 2
3.11 Major or Minor Triad? Exercise 3
3.12 Major or Minor Triad? Exercise 4
3.13 Major or Minor Triad? Exercise 5
3.14 Major or Minor Triad? Exercise 6
3.15 Gsus2 Triad
3.16 Gsus4 Triad
3.17 Building Sus Chords
3.18 Sus2 or Sus4? Exercise 1
3.19 Sus2 or Sus4? Exercise 2
3.20 Sus2 or Sus4? Exercise 3
3.21 Sus2 or Sus4? Exercise 4
3.22 Sus2 or Sus4? Exercise 5
3.23 Sus2 or Sus4? Exercise 6
3.24 Triads in C
3.25 Chord Sequence in C (All Major and Minor Triads)
3.26 Chord Sequence Chord I
3.27 Chord Sequence Chords I & V
3.28 Chord Sequence Chords I & V (Bass & Drums)
3.29 Hear the Changes (Part 1) Exercise 1
3.30 Hear the Changes (Part 1) Exercise 2
3.31 Hear the Changes (Part 1) Exercise 3
3.32 Perfect Cadence (Piano & Guitar)
3.33 Imperfect Cadence (Piano & Guitar)
3.34 Chord Sequence - Imperfect & Perfect Cadences
3.35 Chord Sequence - Chords I & IV
3.36 Chord Sequence - Chords I & IV (Bass & Drums)
3.37 Plagal Cadence (Piano & Guitar)
3.38 Hear the Changes (Part 2) Exercise 1
3.39 Hear the Changes (Part 2) Exercise 2
3.40 Hear the Changes (Part 2) Exercise 3
3.41 Chord Sequence Chords I, IV, & V
3.42 Chord Sequence Chords I, IV, & V (Bass & Drums)
3.43 Hear the Changes (Part 3) Exercise 1
3.44 Hear the Changes (Part 3) Exercise 2
3.45 Hear the Changes (Part 3) Exercise 3
3.46 Hear the Changes (Part 3) Exercise 4
3.47 Chord Sequence Chord vi (Relative Minor)
3.48 Chord Sequence Chord vi (Relative Minor) Bass & Drums
3.49 Chord Sequence Beginning on Chord vi
3.50 Chord Sequence Beginning on Chord vi (Bass & Drums)
3.51 Hear the Changes (Part 4) Exercise 1
3.52 Hear the Changes (Part 4) Exercise 2
3.53 Hear the Changes (Part 4) Exercise 3
3.54 Hear the Changes (Part 4) Exercise 4
3.55 12-Bar Blues in C
3.56 12-Bar Blues in C with a Quick Change
3.57 12-Bar Blues in C with a Long V Chord
3.58 12-Bar Blues in C with a ii-V-I
3.59 12-Bar Blues in D Exercise 1
3.60 12-Bar Blues in Bb Exercise 2
3.61 12-Bar Blues in F Exercise 3
3.62 12-Bar Blues in G Exercise 4
4.01 Melody on Guitar
4.02 Melody with Stepwise Movement in C
4.03 Melody with Stepwise Movement in F
4.04 Melody with Leaps in Bb
4.05 Melody with Leaps in A
4.06 C Major Pentatonic Scale
4.07 Bb Pentatonic Melody
4.08 F Pentatonic Melody
4.09 G Pentatonic Melody
4.10 Transcribing Pentatonic Melodies Exercise 1
4.11 Transcribing Pentatonic Melodies Exercise 2
4.12 Transcribing Pentatonic Melodies Exercise 3
4.13 Transcribing Pentatonic Melodies Exercise 4
4.14 Transcribing Pentatonic Melodies Exercise 5
4.15 Transcribing Pentatonic Melodies Exercise 6
4.16 Call and Response Melody on 12-Bar Blues
4.17 Call and Response Melodies Exercise 1
4.18 Call and Response Melodies Exercise 2
4.19 Call and Response Melodies Exercise 3

EXPLORE TRINITY EBOOKS

ROCK & POP FROM 2018

Trinity's best-selling *Rock & Pop Songbooks from 2018* are available in ebook format for Bass, Drums, Guitar, Keyboards, and Vocals from Initial to Grade 8.

A huge range of Trinity Rock & Pop repertoire is also available as single-piece ebook downloads, including pieces from the songbooks, and extra repertoire that can be used as the own-choice option in the exam.

Scan to explore Rock & Pop ebooks

DRUM KIT EBOOKS

Scan to explore Drum Kit ebooks

Trinity's *Drum Kit Exam Pieces & Exercises from 2020* books cover everything a drummer needs to prepare for the performance and technical work components of Trinity Drum Kit exams, including downloadable demo audio and backing tracks and performance notes.

Also available: *Introducing Drum Kit* parts 1-3 for the early stages of learning, *Sound at Sight Drum Kit*, and *Unpitched Aural Specimen Tests*.

ACOUSTIC GUITAR EBOOKS

Trinity's *Acoustic Guitar Exam Pieces from 2020* books are vital and relevant for today's developing guitarist, and include all the exam pieces for the grades printed in both tablature and standard notation. Inlcudes downloadable demo and backing track audio.

Also available: *Introducing Guitar* for beginner guitarists, *Graded Favourites*, *Scales, Arpeggios & Studies*, and *Aural Specimen Tests*.

Scan to explore Acoustic Guitar ebooks